PERSPECTIVES
for ENTERTAINMENT FACILITIES

遊空間のスケッチパース

レジャー＆アミューズメント施設のためのプレゼンテクニック

KIYOSHI NAKATA

CONTENTS

第1章
エンターテインメント施設のスケッチパース

第3章
エンターテインメント施設のエレメント

第2章
制作のプロセスとノウハウ

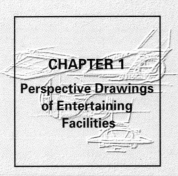

CHAPTER 1
**Perspective Drawings
of Entertaining
Facilities**

CHAPTER 3
**Drawings
of Entertaining
Facilities**

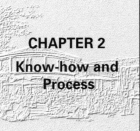

CHAPTER 2
**Know-how and
Process**

はじめに
Preface

仲田 貴代史

ふりかえれば，私は幼いころから絵の好きな子供で，道や塀など，あたりかまわず，よその家の壁にも絵を描いていました。壁の「らくがき」は長い間，残っていて，そこには顔から手，足が生えた人間，空飛ぶ汽車，アニメのキャラクターもどきと，それこそバラバラに描かれていました。絵といっても実物を見て描くというより，頭の中に入っているデータをいっぱいにふくらませて好きかってに描いていたのでしょう。絵の描きはじめなんて，だれでもこんなものじゃないでしょうか。ただひとつ言えるのは，そこに楽しさがあったということです。

学生時代に宮後先生と出会い，夢，イメージを形にする仕事があることを教えられ，パースの素晴らしさと難しさ，またパースの基本的な考え方をいろいろな角度から教わりました。子供のころの生態がばれてしまったのか，夢づくりのためのスケッチを多く描かせてもらったように思います。今は，師の元を離れ，私なりに仕事の上でさまざまなパースを描いていますが，パースというものは，現物を見ながら描くのではなく，まだ形のない予想図を描くわけですから，頭の中にあるイメージの世界を描くことになります。通常，クライアントの頭に浮かんだイメージが自分の頭と手を通過して通訳されるだけのように思われがちですが，実際には自分のフィルターを通して，言葉だけだったイメージをふくらませ，目に見えるものとしていっそうリアルに現実性を帯びたものに変身させる，楽しく手応えのある仕事です。この感覚を，ぜひ皆さんにも味わっていただきたいというのが今回の出版の発端です。

今回，この本に掲載されたような「遊びの空間」を描く時は，クライアントから説明を受けている段階で，その空間に自分自身が入り込んでゆき，その場面の登場人物の一人や，それを眺めている人になりきることが大切だと思っています。たとえば，「通り」のパースを描く時はカフェテラスの椅子に腰掛けている自分がいて，通り行く人や花壇にすわって話しているカップル，マウンティンバイクを走らせる子供たちや，風になびく街路樹，遠くには大道芸人のまわりの人だかりなどがあり，それらを眺めています。こうなれば，そのパースは自ずと雰囲気ができあがってきます。読者の中のプランナーの方は，既にその世界は十分ご理解いただいているはずです。とにかく面倒がらずに手を動かしてみてください。夢が形になったとき，その時の嬉しさ，感動は昔の子供時代のときの心のはずみに匹敵するものと思います。そして描いているときの状態は必ず作品に反映します。いい状態でのプロセスは必ず作品に反映します。逆につまらないという状態もまた作品に影響します。楽しい状態で描いた作品は，見るものにとっても楽しい想いが伝わるものです。

さあ，鉛筆と紙を本の横に準備していただけましたか？ スケッチへの扉を開いていってください。この本の最後のページに至るまでには，その紙の上にたくさんの線が描き込まれていることを願います。

PREFACE

I remember my childhood. I loved to make pictures on roads, walls, and everywhere. My scribbling at that time on walls still remains now. They are a strange man only with his head and limbs, a flying locomotive, heroes of animation, and other things. These picture are not drawings from real life, of course. I drew them using my imagination fully. I would say most children come to draw pictures like this. One thing I notice is that I really enjoyed drawing.

I met Mr. Miyago when I was a student. He showed me a profession to draw perspective and told me how it was wonderful and hard. I learned various aspects and phases of perspective. What youth is used to, ages remember. Giving full play to my imagination in perspectives, I could make my dream come true in drawing. After I finished school many years ago, I started to draw numerous perspectives on my own. As perspectives depend on imagination not on reality, it is nearly fictitious and purely the product of inventiveness. This work clearly shows me results and is to visualizes language of clients realistically through our filter of pictorialization, although some people usually regard it as just interpreting of client's images using hands and heads. I hope readers will enjoy drawing perspective as I do. That is why I was pleased to publish this book.

When you draw perspectives of such amusement facilities as I present in this book, it is important for you to imagine you are in the environment upon explanation of client's explanation. To draw a street scene, imagine you sit on a chair at a cafe on the street, watching kinds riding mountain bicycles, roadside trees bending in the wind, a crowd gathering around street performers, etc. If you make good pictures of a scene in your mind, you will get a feeling of the environments and succeed in drawing it beautifully. Readers who work as architectural project planners will easily get a gist of it in this book. It is desirable for you not to think it is troublesome and boring to use your hands for drawings. You will be so happy and moved to complete a drawing to express your dream, which makes you experience your happy childhood. Your drawing surely reflects your feeling. If you feel good when you work, you will get a splendid drawing. If you feel dull, you just draw a prosaic drawing. Your delight will reach to seers of your drawings, if you are pleased to draw.

Do you have pencils and sheets of paper at hand by this book ? Open your drawing book. I hope you will draw many drawings on your drawing book by the time you finish this book.

Kiyoshi Nakata

監修のことば
Supervisor's Note

宮後 浩

エンターテインメント・スケッチとは，楽しさ，賑やかさ，面白さ，激しさなど，行ってみたくなるような雰囲気が，おもちゃ箱のようにつまった絵。そこにあるのは，抜けるような空の青さ，ジェットコースターのスピード感，ゆるやかな川の流れる音，温泉の湯気の香り，親子連れが手をつないでいる手の感触……，ひとの感覚です。人間は，一見ばらばらに見える感覚を，空間と一体化させて雰囲気として捉えることができます。これを絵として具体化させるのがエンターテインメント・スケッチなのです。もともと断片的な感覚を線に変え，それを積み重ね，交わらせて織り成す一枚のスケッチ。さらにそのスケッチが発想を広げ，ふくらませ，新たな発想へとつながっていきます。

プランナーにとって，このプロセスは避けては通れない部分のひとつです。にもかかわらず"苦手"とするひとが少なくないのが現状です。イメージ通りのスケッチが描けず，かゆいところに手が届かないような苛立ちをおぼえ，つらいことを強いられ

ている思いに駆られる人は意外に多いらしいのです。そんな状態では面白い発想も湧いてこないし，当然，楽しい雰囲気など伝わるはずがありません。スケッチはプロに任せようなどと言う人もいますが，それは最終プレゼンテーション段階での話。考察段階でこんなことを言っていてはプランニングをあきらめたに等しいと私は思っています。発想→考察→スケッチ→新たな発想→考察→スケッチ…永遠に続くループ状のプロセスを途中で断ち切ることはできません。プランナーにとってスケッチは描けて当たり前の技術，自然と身に付くはずの技術なのです。

こういうあきらめかけている人というのは，"絵"としてまとまったものしか見ていません。その"絵"を構成しているディテールや線１本１本を見ようとしない。この線１本を描くことから始めればよいのです。これについてはデッサンをお勧めします。ものを見る力，描く力，そして必要な１本の線を的確に見つけ出す力を身につけるのです。何もデッサン教室

に通う必要はありません。常にものを見，常に手を動かす，これを繰り返し行う作業こそがディテールを作り，バランスのとれたスケッチを形成していくのです。全体をざっくり描ければいいので，細かい部分は必要ないと思っている方も，始まりは１本の線です。きちんと細かい描き込みもできて初めて省略する部分が分かってきて，ざっくり描けるようになるのです。ただ手抜きをしたのでは意味がありません。

この本は，こういう"スケッチは苦手"と思い込んでいる方々のために企画されました。デッサンから部分的なディテール，完成スケッチ例までプロセスを掲載しています。これまでもエンターテインメントに関する写真集，作品集などはたくさん出版されています。素晴らしい作品ばかりです。ではそのスケッチを描くプロセスは？　となると雰囲気の描き方なんて教えられないよとみんな口を揃えて言います。それはひとえに描くという作業部分と，何を描くかという発想の部

A drawing of an entertaining facility look like a gigantic toy box filled with a cheerful, merry, amusing, and exciting atmosphere, which makes us feel like going there. In such a facility, the sky is high and blue, a roller coaster is thrilling, and water flows make soothing sound. You smell steamy air of a hot spring and feel touch of children's hands. You can sense various feelings in a drawing of the entertaining facility. Portraying our feelings, lines and lines weave a drawing and stimulate our imaginations.

Architectural planners cannot do without drawing ability. But many of them tell that they are not good at drawing. Contrary to general belief, I heard that many planners continue planning, dissatisfied with drawings for their image. If it is true, they will not probably create good plans nor express joyful feelings of a project in drawings. Some planers

ask specialists to draw perspectives but they place an order at the final stage of planning. I think if a planner give his drawing work to specialists, he means to give up planning. A planner should work in a long circle of process in which he study, think, sketch, restudy, rethink, re-sketch, on and on….

I would like to make one thing clear that planners deserve to draw or they naturally learn how to draw while working.

If one nearly gives up drawing, he just see a whole drawing and does not see details and lines. But just one stroke of drawing will give him a breakthrough. Of course it must be bitter for him to practice sketching. In doing so, he will learn how to observe, express, and select one right line. He does not have to take a sketching course. A sharp and watchful eye and persevering work will give you skills and ability to draw details to make good

composition of drawing. Some people may say there is not time to practice sketching. What many of you are asked to do is to draw total and rough drawings. But we must draw details anyway. You have to start with drawing one line. Unless you study and work for details of a drawing, you will not be able to understand how to simplify it. If there is some corner-cutting in your drawing, it will impress nobody.

I planned this book for anyone who find it hard to draw. It covers from the basic sketch to various details and renderings. We know there are many books about perspective drawings and photographs of entertaining facilities. They are all excellent. But, the process of drawing is still neglected there. Almost all renderers tell that showing how to express an atmosphere is impossible. I think it is because they confuse what and how. Sure, no one can show what to

分をひとつのものに捉えているからに他なりません。何を描くかなんて教えられないし，ましてやプランナーの方に教えるなどというのはおこがましい話です。しかし，作業の部分は違います。ある程度のルールの中でできている領域です。技術なら見て練習できるし，勉強もできるし…後は慣れ（繰り返し）です。スケッチが描けるくらいで，あたかも巨匠のように"秘伝のテクニック"などと後生大事に言っていても宝の持ち腐れ。見て勉強になるのなら全部見せてしまいましょうということで今回の運びとなりました。

著者の仲田君はわが社に十数年在籍し，特にエンターテインメント関連については常にご指名で発注を受けていた人物です。独立した今でもその作品のクオリティーは高く，幅広い活動を続けています。彼のスケッチは，技術もさることながら人間性からくる深い味わいとやさしい香りを醸し出しています。この部分が個性となって人々の心に，よりいっそうエンターテインメントの楽しさ，面白さを印

象づけているのかもしれません。個性は技術ではないので真似しても仕方がありませんし，実際，各個人のもっているものが否応無しに表面化される部分ですから真似ることもできません。日常生活での考え方，行動のすべてがそのスケッチに表れるのです。そういう意味では，言葉を話すように，文章を書くように，スケッチも無意識のうちにその人となりが表現されているということにもなるでしょう。これは一足飛びに本を見て学べることではありません。一日一日をどう生きているか，経験の蓄積であり，意識の持ち方であり，感性の鋭さの問題です。机に座って勉強しても，どうなるものでもありません。この本では技術を，より高いレベルのテクニックを勉強してください。

彼の技術を余すことなく網羅したこの本は，必ずや多くのプランナーを助け，新たな発想の泉へと導く"地図"となることをお約束します。

〈みやご・ひろし／コラムデザインセンター代表〉

draw. It must be hard to teach it planners. But we know everyone has his own specialty. If there are any rules, there must be ways to use them. Studying and learning technique by following examples of others is not difficult. Practice makes perfect. Once you learn steps to it, you will find it easy to reach it again.

Mr.Nakata, the author of this book, worked more than ten years for our company and was commissioned to draw drawings of entertaining facilities for a number of clients who love his work. Later he set up his firm and high quality of his work enhanced his reputation. He extended his work in various fields and his style reflects his gentleness. His individuality may appeal to people through his work, which is expressed energetically in his drawing of entertaining facilities.

Making a model of someone's technique is worth while but copying someone's character style is no use. Individuality makes one's style.

Your ways of thinking and acting influence your style. In that sense, your drawing style is what you are, as well as your speaking and writing. Your drawings involve your personal history, experience, consciousness, and sensibility. You cannot learn how to draw if you are swotting up knowledge. Use your brain, eyes, and ears to see much of the world. Gather data and information. Keep your curiosity active to all things in nature.

This book comprise experience and technique of Mr. Nakata. I believe it will assist many planners as guide maps for sources of new ideas.

Hiroshi Miyago

第1章

エンターテインメント施設のスケッチパース
Perspective Drawings of Entertaining Facilities

夢と現実の狭間をビジュアル化する
Visualizing Dream, Reality, and the In-between

これまで約20年。数多くのパースを描いてきました。パースという仕事の領域が，おぼろげながら見えてきた頃から描き続けていると言ってもいいかもしれません。

当初，パースといえば，建築の設計者自身が確認の意味も含めて描く，まさしく建物の完成予想図であり，きちんとそろった図面通りの正確さを追求するものが大半だったと思います。描く用具も限られており，コンピューターまで使うようになる業界になろうとは，当時，予想もつかなかったことです。もちろん今日でも，この正攻法での描法を中心にパースと呼びますが，それ以外にも幅広い領域のものをパースと呼ぶようになりました。その一つが，今回のエンターテインメント・スケッチを含むイメージスケッチです。これは「図」というよりむしろ「絵」であり，正確な設計も確定しない段階での出番が多いパースと言えます。図面もないのに何を描くのか

…。これから図面になるもの，頭の中にあるもの，つまり"イメージ"を描くのです。

では，そのイメージとは何でしょうか？ それは設計者（プランナー）の想いであり，この建物（プラン）のテーマにほかなりません。その想いは，設計者（プランナー）の言葉を通して，雰囲気としてわれわれに伝えられます。それを的確な場面を使って，感覚を具現化したものこそがイメージスケッチなのです。ここで最も重要なのは図法を守るだけではなく，感覚を伝える動き，空気の流れを描くことです。そのためには，少しぐらいデフォルメがあっても一向に構いません。気持ちが入り過ぎるあまりの行き過ぎというのはスケッチではよくあることです。もちろん，優れたテクニックも必要です。しかし，気持ちの込もっていないテクニックは単なる作業であり，雰囲気を伝える感覚までを描き出すことは不可能です。気持ちの上では，すでにその場に立っているく

For about twenty years, I have been drawing many perspective drawings. When I started my career, even definition and domain of perspective drawings were still vague in Japan. Perspective drawings were at that time drawn by architects or architectural designers themselves to show just completed images of their projects precisely upon architectural drawings. In those days, art supplies for perspectives were in short and nobody could expect that computers were introduced to drawing later. Majority of designers draw by orthodox method of such accurate perspective drawings.

Perspective drawings are diverse. Readers will notice in this book such diversity. Drawings of entertaining facilities are good examples. They are quite artistic or in fine-art style rather than mere illustrations. Many of them were drawn at the early stage of architectural projects when draftings were not

finished. How drawings are made regardless of drafts is very interesting. I draw images using imagination or brain child.

Then, what are the images I use ? They are ideas of planners or themes of the plans. We can catch and understand the ideas through words of planners. We embody and use ideas. We call them image drawings. Most important thing is to express the air in a drawing to show a feeling, not just to keep precise perspective. For that reason, I sometimes do not care distortion. Distortion often occurs when we emphasize something in our perspective drawings. Of course, I use various techniques to make use of distortion and deformation. But mechanical technique cannot always convey feeling and atmosphere. Technique is just technique. We should have a sense of presence that we feel as if we were really in the

らいの臨場感を自分で感じて描きたいものです。

今回は，特に気持ちを優先させているエンターテインメント・スケッチを中心に掲載しています。気持ちが先を行くあまり，「少し歪んでいるのでは？」と思うくらい勢いのあるものを集めました。皆さんがご覧になって，行ってみたい，体験してみたいと思っていただけるものはあるでしょうか？
掲載作品はあらゆるジャンルから抜粋しています。

1．日常的な生活の側にある憩い…
　　一般公園, プール, レストラン, ショッピングモール,
　　ストリート, 展示場
2．非日常的なリゾート感覚のやすらぎ…
　　リゾートホテル, 農場公園, 遊園地, スキー場
3．刺激的な感情の高ぶり…
　　パチンコ店, ゲームセンター, カラオケボックス
4．その他…町おこしなどの企画物件

これらは，いずれも私自身の好奇心を満足させる，現実から10cmくらい浮いた世界，つまり，現実と夢との狭間をビジュアル化させています。いまだこの世に存在しない夢を臨場感たっぷりに描く…素晴らしい仕事です。ただし夢は一瞬です。この夢は刹那的に頭に浮かぶほんの一瞬のイメージですから，いかに素早く短時間で描きとめるかということも重要な事項になります。そんな時に図法や何かにとらわれている暇はないのです。短時間で刹那的な一瞬のイメージ…"ひらめき"を想いと勢いで描く。これがまさにイメージスケッチと言えるでしょう。そしてその"ひらめき"の具現化が，またさらなる"ひらめき"を生む可能性を秘めているのです。ページをめくる度にあなたにもその楽しさと感動を味わっていただきたい，そう願います。

place of a project when we see a drawing

In this book, I gathered many drawings of entertaining facilities. I love to choose expressive pieces of work, many of which may give readers a sense of distortion in perspectives. I hope these works make readers feel like going or experiencing the places and buildings I drew.

This book covers various types of projects and there are following four themes.

1) Relaxation in everyday life ; park, swimming pool, restaurant, shopping mall, street, and exhibition
2) Comfort in resorts ; resort hotel, farm park, amusement park, and ski ground
3) Emotion and excitement ; pachinko parlor, game center, and karaoke rooms
4) Unique projects and events such as a mikoshi (a Shinto festival artifact)

Above-mentioned four key concepts belong to what I call the world of ten centimeter floating reality in which I have been interested. I draw real world, unreal world, and the in between. With the use of a sense of presence, I draw unborn dream world. It is a splendid work. Such dream is momentary, so it is important to jot down dream instantaneously. Sometimes there is no time for pondering correct perspective orthography. Drawing intuitional image on the spot off the cuff is nothing but image sketching I mentioned. Intuition calls for inspiration and one inspiration makes another. I hope readers will be impressed and enjoy themselves, turning pages of this book one by one.

マリンスポーツ＆リゾート
Marine Sports & Resort

地域によって四季の様相が違う日本において，「リゾート」といえば，海へ，山へと都会の喧騒から離れるというイメージが一般的です。やはり人間のもつ自然回帰の心が，山の緑，海の青，抜けるほど高く澄みきった空を求めるからなのでしょうか？リゾート関連のスケッチ依頼を受ける時，最初は大いなる「夢」の世界を想像します。クライアントも初期段階では，予算の細かい部分まで煮つまっていないことも手伝って，夢いっぱいの状態ですが，幾度か打ち合わせをしていくうちに，次第にその姿は，より現実的なものに姿を変えていくことになります。今回の作品は初期段階のもので，わたし自身の夢いっぱいの期待も折り混ぜて描いたものです。日中，太陽の下でアクティブなスポーツに熱中し，疲れた体が，木陰で飲むトロピカルドリンクの味を，よりさわやかな味に感じさせるビーチサイド。夜は少しゴージャスな服を身にまとい，リッチな気分でディナーを楽しんだ後，おしゃれなラウンジホールでバンドの生演奏とカクテルを楽しむ。日常から解き放たれた心地よい解放感を十分に味わいたい大人の楽園を描いた作品にしたつもりです。

1. サンドバギーによる浜辺のスポーツレジャー　Sport leisure by a sand buggy

2. K マリーナのヨットハーバー計画案　The yacht harbor project of K marina

3. ジェットスキーによるマリンスポーツ　Marine sport by a jet ski

4. Kホテル・磯辺からの外観
The external appearance of the K hotel from the seaside

5. Kホテル・ビーチ側のデッキラウンジ　The seaside deck lounge of the K hotel

6. Kホテル・トロピカルガーデン内の滝のあるプール　The tropical garden's pool of K hotel

7. ナイトクルージング中のバーラウンジ　The bar lounge in the cruising ship

8. トロピカルガーデン内の滝のある空中テラス。ジャングルの向こう側に海が見える　The sky terrace in the tropical garden of the K hotel

9. Kホテル・ジャズ演奏中のサパークラブ　The supper club in the K hotel

Four seasons in Japan make different landscapes in different seasons. For Japanese people, resorts generally mean places near mountains or the sea far from noise of big busy cities. I think we are by nature enchanted to the nature represented by green mountains, blue sea, high clear sky, and so on.

When I draw drawings of resort projects, I imagine big fantasy world. Clients also have dreams about the projects before they decide the details of the budget in the early stage of the projects. After several meetings with the clients, the images of the project shape themselves gradually.

Most works of mine I present in this book are early ones drawn by my dream and enthusiasm. In those dreams, figures play sports hard during daytime and drink tropical drink at night under trees on the beach. Sometimes figures wear gorgeous clothing, enjoy dinner in a rich atmosphere, drink tasty cocktails and dance to the music by a band in a ballroom. I drew a paradise of adults who want to release themselves, escaped from reality.

スキー＆マウンテンリゾート
Ski & Mountain Resort

1．スキーゲレンデでのスノーボーディング　Snowboarding in the skiing ground

As a planner, I actually joined this ski resort project from the beginning. Here are sketches and plan boards for presentation of cottages and the main lodge. Basic concept of this resort project is based upon a Canadian mountain village where people enjoy hiking and cycling in conifer forests in summer. Sound of stroke always fills tennis courts. In winter, skiers and snow boarders enjoy themselves in this place covered with snow and they spend the night near the fireplace with glasses of wine in their hands. I drew those images and atmosphere in my drawings. Since I was a guest of this lodge for the first time, I have often visited and stayed there for a long time. It was a great pleasure that I made the owner's dream visible as an intimate member of his project.

3. スノーモビルによるウインタースポーツ風景
Winter auto-sport by a snowmobile

2. カナディアンビレッジ計画案(冬景色)。中央がメーンホテル，周囲に旧ロッジとコテージ群
Bird's-eye view of the Canadian Village project in winter

このプランは，企画段階でプランナーとしてかかわったものです。メーンロッジを中心としたコテージ全体のプレゼンテーションのために作成したスケッチとイメージプランボードです。基本的なイメージは，カナダの山あいの村。夏は緑濃い針葉樹の連立する森でハイキング，サイクリングを楽しむ人。テニスコートからはストロークの音が聞こえてくる。冬は，もちろんスキーにスノーボード。見渡す限り雪，雪，雪の銀世界をエキサイティングに滑り降り，ロッジ内では暖かい暖炉を囲んでワイン片手に楽しい夜を過ごす……，そういう雰囲気を描き込んでみました。

もともと，このロッジとのおつき合いは，仕事を頼まれる以前から，わたし自身が客として利用したときより始まっており，わたしの中に最初から仕事以上の思いがあったことも手伝って，オーナーとともに夢を形にしてゆけることは実に素晴らしいことでした。

4. メーンホテル内のクラシカルなレストラン
View of the classic style restaurant in the main hotel

CANADIAN VILLAGE

5. カナディアンビレッジ計画案のコンセプトボード　The concept board of the Canadian Village project

6. カナディアンビレッジ最終案(夏景色)　The final plan of the Canadian Village project

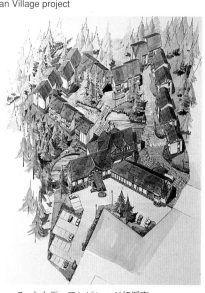

7. カナディアンビレッジ初期案
The early plan of the Canadian Village project

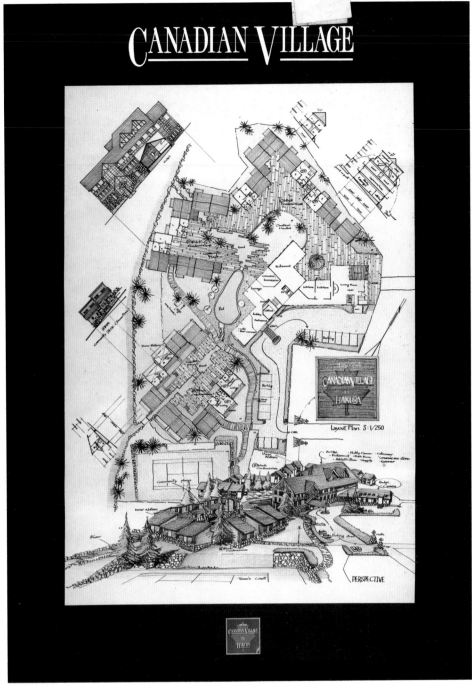

CANADIAN VILLAGE

8. 配置図と全体デザインをビジュアルに表現したプレゼンテーションボード
The presentation board of the site plan and whole design

9. 屋外に設置されたジャクジー　View of the outdoor jacuzzi

10. 暖炉のあるリビング　The living room with fireplace in the cottage

11. スキーゲレンデから見たカナディアンビレッジとその周辺全景
Whole view of the Canadian Village and surrounding environment from the skiing ground

ファームパーク（農場公園）
Farm Park

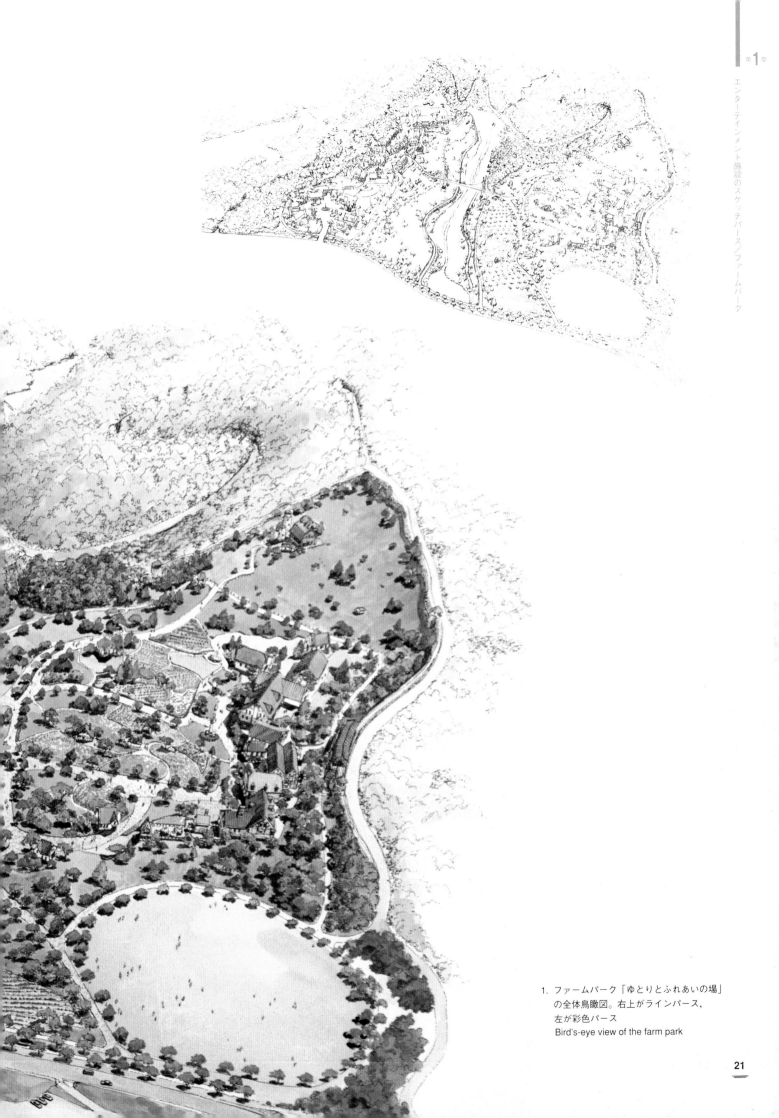

1. ファームパーク「ゆとりとふれあいの場」
の全体鳥瞰図。右上がラインパース，
左が彩色パース
Bird's-eye view of the farm park

2. ファームパークのエントランス前に設けられた広場。近郊農家の収穫物を販売する出店が並ぶ　View of the plaza in front of the farm park entrance

3. ファームパーク内の散策路　The promenade for walking in the farm park

これらは，実際に都市近郊の広大な雑木林に作られた農場公園です。
「石だたみの遊歩道をのんびりと歩いて行くと，四季おりおりの彩りを見せる花畑，その向こうには動物たちがたわむれている。農家の家と思われる赤い屋根の建物に入って行くとチーズの香りが立ちこめて……」。そんなイメージが次々と頭をよぎり，仕事でありながら，日々忙しさに追われるわたしの生活に潤いを与えてくれました。こういう公園が都市郊外にあるというのが，このプランの素晴らしさの一要因です。ちょっと足を延ばすだけで日常の喧騒から抜け出して，牧歌的な空間へと移動できるというのは素晴らしいことです。わたし自身も，描いているだけで自然に帰れる思いがしました。

4. ファームパーク内の泉のあるプラザ　The plaza with fountain in the farm park

5. クラシックカーを展示したファームパーク内のホール　The display room with classical cars in the farm park

6. ファームパーク・ハーブガーデンでのバーベキュー風景　The barbecue scene of the herb garden in the farm park

7. ファームパーク内で作られたソーセージ，チーズ，地ビールを中心としたメニューのビアレストラン
Interior view of the brewery restaurant in the farm park

Here are works for a real project of farm park surrounded by thicket in a suburb of the big city. I had images for this park like this.... Strolling quietly along a paved promenade, people find flower fields of seasonal flowers and animals over there. Entering a farm house with a red roof, they smell cheese..., such imagination gave me a soothing feeling while I was working on this project. I like such a park in suburban. Extending our trip to the countryside is wonderful experience. I myself felt relaxed working on theses drawings.

アミューズメントパーク（遊園地）
Amusement Park

スリル満点のジェットコースター，ワイルドな急流すべり，楽しい音楽が聞こえてくるメリーゴーラウンド，空と地面が勢いよく入れ替わるゴンドラ，恐いもの見たさのおばけ屋敷……。遊園地はまさに笑い声でいっぱいのおもちゃ箱です。いつの時代でも，子供はもちろんヤングからアダルト，シルバーまで，時間が経つのも忘れて遊べる場所です。そんな夢の世界を描いたこの作品は，アミューズメント・スケッチの代表格と言えるのではないでしょうか。無邪気な子供の心を忘れないで，大人もいっしょに楽しめるものを心に描いています。

1. 遊園地の楽しさを演出するメリーゴーラウンド　Detail of the merry-go-round

2. Hパークのバラ園入り口計画案　The entrance project of the rose garden in the H amusement

3. 上部にお化け屋敷を設けたスリックカート　The slick cart course under the haunted house

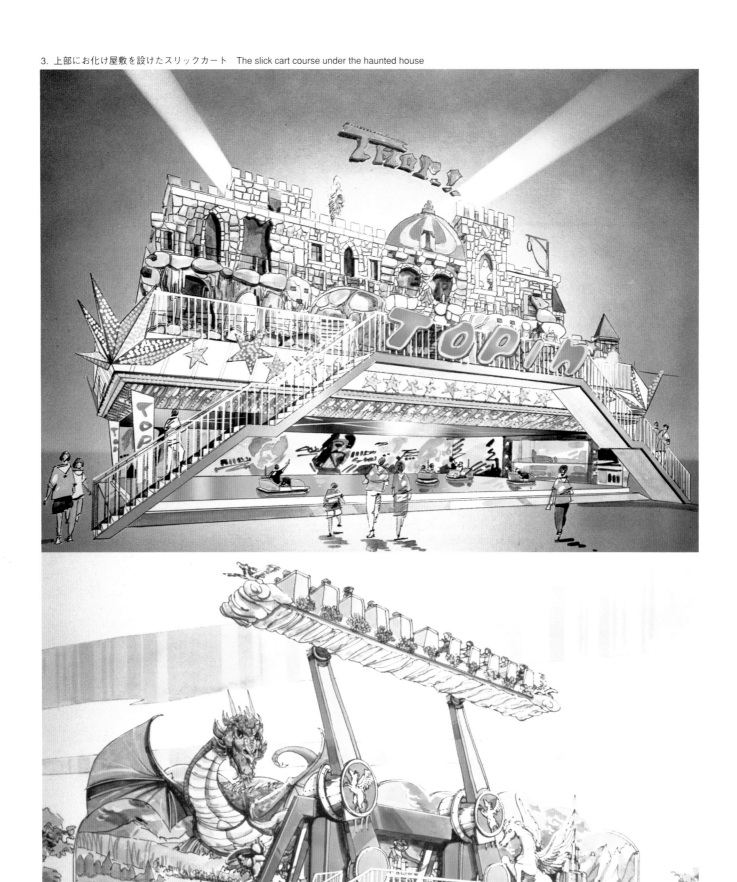

4. ダイナミックな楽しさを演出するフライングカーペット　The ride naming "the flying carpet"

5. 遊園地のゲートとゲームゾーンの全景　　Whole view of the gate and game arcade

6. 西部劇の町並みを模したゲームゾーン・ウェスタンカーニバル　　The game arcade naming "Western carnival"

7. 同じく西部劇の町並みを模したゲームゾーン　　The game arcade naming "Western carnival"

There are thrilling roller coaster, a wild water slider, a merry-go-round to merry music, gondola moving abruptly up and down, a haunted house stimulating your curiosity, and so on in an amusement park. It is a kind of big toy box filled with laughter and enjoyment. In any period, kids, young people, grown-ups, and elder people devoted themselves in playing there. These drawings represent a dream world of an amusement park. Awaking a child in my mind, I drew something to please adults for my drawings.

8. Hパークのバラ園リニューアル計画全景　The renewal project of rose garden in the H amusement park

9. Oパークのジェットコースター乗り場　The roller coaster platform in the O amusement park

10. Hパークのバラ園に設けられたメリーゴーラウンド
The merry-go-round in the rose garden of the H amusement park

11. Hパークの山頂に設けられたジェットコースター全景　The roller coaster on the hill in the H amusement park

12. 林の中を走るOパークのジェットコースター走路　The roller coaster running inside the woods in the O amusement park

1. 倉庫を改修したK町のコミュニティー施設計画案　The community center project by remodelling the warehouse in the K town

観光レジャー施設（町おこし施設）
Tourists Leisure Facility

こういった作品は，古くからそこに根付いているものを壊さないで共生できることを企画し，また新たな空気を送り込み，より今日的で生き生きとした活気ある町にすることを念頭に進めています。その町の特産物やもともとの名所，歴史的な背景，自然発生的な景観等をおろそかに扱うことはできません。ですから，それを活かし，より多くの人々に注目してもらえるものにするために，知的欲求をかきたてられるだけでなく，どこかノスタルジックな気分にさせられるイメージを持ち合せたものを意識して描きました。より正確な街の情報を得て，歴史的知識の把握も求められますので綿密な打ち合わせが必要になってきます。

2. 町内で夏に催される「だんじりまつり」　The summer festival scene in the town

3. 和風デザインでまとめられたコミュニティー施設の宿泊棟計画案　Japanese style lodgings project in the K town

4. 宿泊施設の前に設けられた広場での朝市　The morning market in front of lodging

5. コミュニティー施設背後の庭に面した和風ガーデンテラス　Japanese style garden terrace in the rear of community center

6. 地元特産品をメニューに加えたコミュニティー施設内のレストランホール　Interior view of the restaurant with special products in the community center

Utilizing local colors and the environment, these facilities for tourists were planned to revitalize and keep harmony with local towns. Principal products, sight seeing spots, historical background, and other spontaneous generational landscapes were also considered for such projects, which stir up our intellectual curiosity and nostalgia. I drew landscapes, depending upon correct data of a town, having meeting with the staff again and again for historical investigation.

7. コミュニティー施設内の民芸品展示コーナー
Display area of the folk craft in the community center

8. コミュニティー施設内の特産品販売コーナー
Retail area of the special products in the community center

9. 宿泊施設のフロントとロビー
The front counter and lobby in the lodging

屋内型テーマパーク
Indoor Amusement Park

新しいタイプのアミューズメントスポットとして、屋内型テーマパークがあります。都市型テーマパークとも呼ばれ、これまでの「遊園地は郊外の広大な土地が必要である」という常識を覆し、街のど真ん中に作られる遊園地です。街中ということは、基本的にスペースが狭いわけですから、屋内型のものが中心になります。屋内の乗り場から乗り込み、走っている間の一部は屋外を通過して、また最後は屋内に戻ってくるようなジェットコースターもこの類になります。青空の下で思いきり遊ぶというタイプとは異なり、映像や音を駆使したSF映画の中に飛び込んだような不思議な世界を体感できる、屋内型ならではの雰囲気をこの作品に表現してみました。

これらのスケッチパースは構想段階のもので、わたし自身の発想でプランしたり、デザインしたりできる余裕のあるものでしたので、幼いころから興味のある「冒険」をテーマに、ハイテクを駆使した近未来の宇宙空間、神秘的な海底や遺跡を探検する場面をイメージしています。

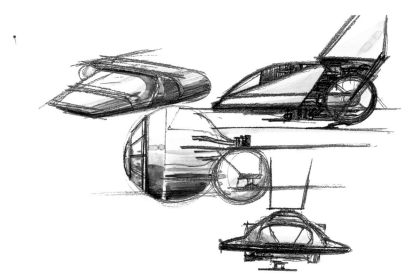

1. 宇宙船タイプ遊具のデザインスケッチ
Design drawings of the spacecraft type play machine

2. 要塞をイメージしたテーマパークの入り口ゲート計画案　The entrance gate project of the theme park imaging a fortress

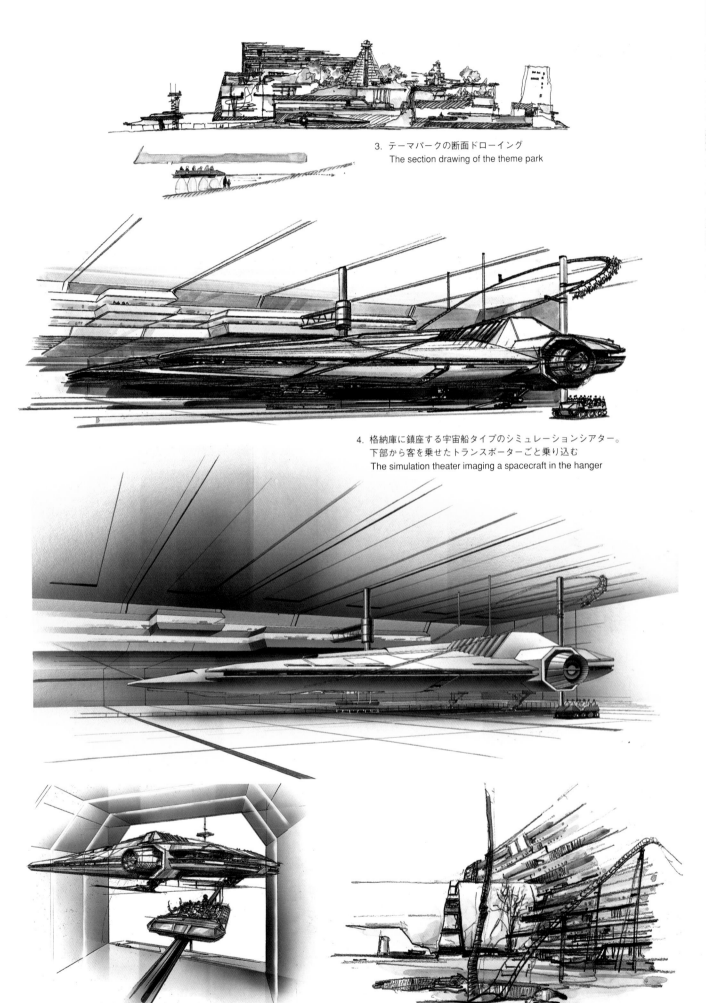

3. テーマパークの断面ドローイング
The section drawing of the theme park

4. 格納庫に鎮座する宇宙船タイプのシミュレーションシアター。
下部から客を乗せたトランスポーターごと乗り込む
The simulation theater imaging a spacecraft in the hanger

5. トランスポーターから見た宇宙船タイプのシミュレーションシアター
View of the simulation theater from the transportation machine

6. 遺跡のある穴に入り込んでいくジェットコースターの軌道走路
The track of the roller coaster dropping the ruins hole

7. 中央アメリカ風の建物で構成されたサブゲート　The subgate of the theme park imaging Latin America

8. 移動のためのトランスポーターの動きに噴水が連動し，ライトアップされる
Transportation machines linking fountains and lightings

9. 海底都市をイメージしたゾーンのジェットコースター　The roller coaster in the sea bottom city zone

10. 海上要塞・ダストアイランドからの亀甲形Uボートによる脱出　Scene of escaping from the sea fortress by the U type boat

11. 海上要塞・ダストアイランド内の急流を下るアドベンチャーボート
Scene of the shooting the rapid by the adventure boat in the sea fortress

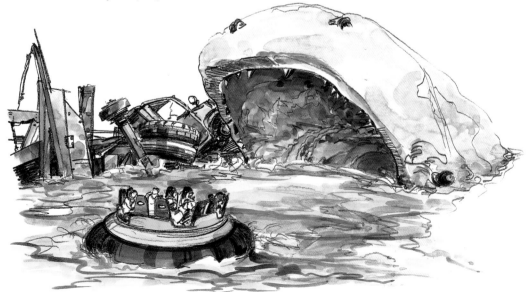

12. 鯨風の巨大怪獣に飲み込まれそうになるアドベンチャーボート　Scene of escaping from the big whale by the adventure boat

13. 海底都市ゾーンに向かう潜水艦型トランスポーター　The submarine type transportation to the sea bottom city

14. 遺跡ゾーン内のジェットコースターとパビリオンショップ
　　The roller coaster and pavilion shops in the ruins zone

Indoor amusement park is a trendy amusement facility and is also called a urban theme park. It is built in the midst of a city, overthrowing common sense that a amusement park needs a vast site in a suburb. As it is located in the city, it is small with indoor amusement. For example, an indoor roller coaster starts from the indoor platform, goes partly outside of the park, and returns the indoor platform again. Different from ordinary coaster in which people enjoy outdoor feeling under blue sky, the indoor coaster makes us feel like we were in a sci-fi movie, with its splendid effect of sound and vision. I dew characteristics of the indoor amusement park, using imagination freely to create anything upon a theme of adventure that I have loved since I was a child. High-tech space ship, mysterious sea bottom and ruins are among my favorite objects.

15. 遺跡ゾーンを巡るジェットコースター
The roller coaster circulating through the ruins zone

16. 遺跡ゾーンの滝をくぐり抜けるトロッコ型コースター　The truck type roller coaster passing the falls in the ruins zone

1. Sパーク内に計画されたアクア遊園地の噴水の島　The fountain island of aqua-park in the S amusement park

プール＆アクアレジャー
Swimming & Aqua Leisure

プールといえば夏というイメージがありましたが、最近では屋内型のものが増え、季節、天候を問わず、楽しめるようになりました。泳ぐという目的だけでなく、大型滑り台で遊んだり、水流の流れる海を体感したり、大きな噴水、水の中のアスレチックを楽しんだりと、まさに水の遊園地です。また、飲食店等のレストルーム、スパなどを複合させた施設も出現し、新しいタイプの娯楽施設としての地位を確立しています。子供から大人まで、ファミリーでもカップルでも友達同士でも遊べる、身近なスポットとして今後も注目される要素がいっぱいです。

水に入るときは裸に近い状態になることから、のびのびとした大胆な行動が生まれるチャンスが多くなります。そんな開放的な雰囲気と楽しい感じが表現できればと思って描いています。

2. Sパーク内に設けられたトロピカルなプールサイドのウオータースライド
The water slide by the side of tropical pool in the S amusement park

3. Sパーク内のアクアアスレチック・ガーデン　The aqua-athletic garden in the S amusement park

4. トロピカルガーデン内のウオーターフォールと屋外ジャクジー
The water falls and outdoor jacuzzi in the tropical garden

Today swimming pools are used all year round regardless of season and weather, for many of them are built indoor. In old times however, they were used mostly in summer. Now people come to swimming pools for not only swimming but also sliding, floating, doing water athletic in water stream, water surprise, and so on. Indoor swimming pools are like water amusement parks. In fact some swimming pools are built as new sports complexes with restaurants, rest lounges, and spas. Children, adults, family, and young couples enjoy themselves here. I think we can be bolder when we put on swim wear, steeped in a sense of freedom. I would like to express such openness in my drawings of swimming pools and so-called aqua leisure centers.

5. Aアクアパレスの内部風景　Interior view of the A aqua-palace

6. O町福祉センター内の室内プール計画案　The indoor pool project of O town welfare center

7. Nパーク内に設けられた滝のあるレストルーム　The resting room with falls in the N amusement park

8. Sパークのアクアゾーン全景イラスト
Whole view of the aqua-zone in the S amusement park

9. 屋内型プールのプールサイド　The poolside of the indoor type pool

10. 屋内型プールのレストテラス
The resting area of the indoor type pool

スパ&温泉
Spas & Hot Springs

1. Nスパパークの滝のある大浴場計画案　The big bathroom project with falls in the N spa park

ストレス蔓延の現代社会で、「健康産業＝癒しのための施設」を語るとき、スパの要素を除いて考えることは困難です。これほどまでに今日的なものはありません。以前なら銭湯あるいは少し遠くの温泉旅館でも、なかなか充実したスパを体験することは不可能でしたが、現在ではそれを専門とした施設がたくさん登場して、健康産業として発展的展開をみせています。

スパの施設は、お湯自体の種類の多さもさることながら、国別のイメージで演出したり、音楽や光の差し込み方に趣向をこらした浴場や、打たせ湯、ジャクジーなど水流に工夫を施した浴槽など、疲れを癒すということにとどまらず、わくわくする要素までを持ち併せています。子供たちがプール感覚で楽しむ場を、大人たちはサウナやマッサージなどで「体と心」をリフレッシュさせる空間を意識して描いたつもりです。

2. 洞窟温泉内の鍾乳石風浴場
The bathroom of stalactite grotto in the cave hot spring

3. 噴水に囲まれたジャクジー浴場　The jacuzzi bathroom surrounded fountains

4. ○町福祉センター内の大浴場計画案
The big bathroom project of O town welfare center

5. 洞窟温泉内の階段テラス状になった浴槽群　The bathrooms of terrace style in the cave hot spring

When we talk about health or healing industry, we should not omit facilities of spas and hot springs in stressful modern society of Japan. These are old and new. In those days, it was not easy to use spas in public bathes or in even hot spring resort in a suburb. Recently, we have a number of spa facilities with its related healing equipments and facilities which are easily accessible.

The spa facilities demonstrate hot water of different areas and countries and have environmental devices of music and light. There are water falls, jacuzzis, and other exciting bathes. Children play with hot water there as they do in a swimming pool, and adults relax by sauna, massage, etc. I dew such refreshing feeling of this type of facilities.

イベント＆エキシビション
Events & Exhibition

1. Wパーク内の盆踊りイベントパビリオン入り口ゲート　The entrance gate of the event pavilion in the W amusement park for the Bon Festival dance

2. イベントパビリオン内部の地元出店ブース
　The booths of local shops in the event pavilion

昔は，イベントといえば町のお祭りぐらいのものでしたが，最近は自治体や地域産業からのバックアップも手伝って，パレードやバザー，スポーツ大会等々，数多くのイベントが繰り広げられています。その目的はさまざまですが，賑やかで楽しい雰囲気のものであることは共通しています。
こういったイベントの作品では，常設の決まった建築物が登場する機会は少なく，華やかな仮設のステージ，人の集まっている出店，風に勢いよくなびくフラッグ，大きな目印にもなるアーチ，ブースが，その場面を演出し盛り上げます。そのひとつひとつの小道具たちも重要ですが，ここでは"人"が主役であり，実際に人の動きが重要なポイントです。人が集まっていることを表現するコツは，ごちゃごちゃとたくさん描くこと。閑散とした会場では賑やかさは表現できません。

3. Jイベント会場内に設けられたフリーマーケットゾーン
The free market zone in the J event assembly hall

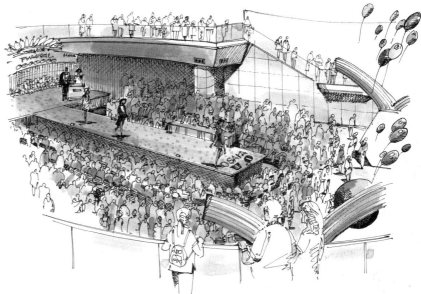

4. Jイベント会場内で行われたファッションショー風景
Scene of the fashion show in the J event assembly hall

5. Jイベント会場内で開催されたコンサート風景
Scene of the music concert in the J event assembly hall

6. Aパーク内におけるパレード風景　Scene of the parade in the A musement park

7. Dフェアーの敷地に飾られた龍のフロートとイベントパビリオン
The event pavilion and dragon display on the ∧D fair

8. Dフェアーのパビリオン内部展示とショップ　The display and shops in the event pavilion

9. アトリウム吹き抜けを利用したステージとフリーマーケット　Scene of stage show and free market in the atrium

10. イベントパビリオン内の企業展示ブース　The display booth of business in the event pavilion

11. T記念館内部のシアターホール　The theater hall in the T memorial building

In the old days, festivals were few of exciting events in our daily life. Now, sometimes backed up by municipal corporations, we have lots of events, such as parades, bazaars, sports events, and so on. They have different aims but have a joyful atmosphere in common. For those events, there are few standing equipments and facilities. Around temporary stages, various stands, banners, arches, and booths, people gather in crowds. These details are essential but figures are most important in drawings of events. To express bustle of events effectively, I drew jumbled scenes of events. When we draw events, we must keep in our mind that fewer figures are less impressive.

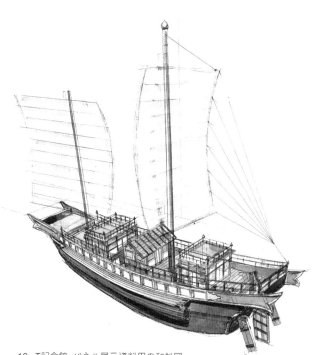

12. T記念館・パネル展示資料用の和船図
The pannel display of Japanese ship in the T memorial building

13. イベントにおける地域紹介展示ゾーン計画案
The display zone project of local area at the event

14. P・T博覧会における東京展示ブース計画案
The display booth project of Tokyo at the P・T exposition

15. A展示ホール内部のキャラクターゾーン　The theme character zone in the A exhibition hole

16. B展示ホールの焼き物展示販売コーナー
The display and retail area of ceramic ware in the B exhibition hole

17. 同じくB展示ホールの焼き物実演体験コーナー
The demonstration area of making ceramic ware in the B exhibition hole

ショッピング＆レストラン街
Shopping Malls & Restaurants

1. Oショッピングモールの東南アジアゾーン計画案　The Southeast Asia zone at the O shopping mall project

日常生活のすぐそばにあって，気持ちがワクワクするもの…，特に女性の方に多いと思いますが，ショッピングというのは手軽に気分をリフレッシュできる方法のひとつではないでしょうか。そんな空間に，楽しい演出がなされていたらどうでしょう？　その場所に行くだけで楽しいショッピングスペースがあったら，やはり自然と人が集まると思います。そういう思いを込めてこの作品を描きました。今回の作品は，ストリート全体でアジアの街を感じさせる賑やかな市場の雰囲気を表現しました。活気があってパワフルなイメージに統一したつもりです。店内はその個々の店舗の個性を生かした内装で特徴づけています。そこに行けば，「食」と「買い物」を通じて異国を味わえるような空間を感じてもらえれば最高です。

2. 中国物産店コーナー　The Chinese goods area

3. Sマーケット・外観デザイン計画案　The external appearance project of S market

4. Oショッピングモールのラテンアメリカ・レストラン街
The Latin America restaurant street in the O shopping mall

5. ショッピング街で買った食材を調理して食べさせてくれるレストラン
The restaurant, cooking food which bought in the shopping mall

6. Rレストランの外観デザイン計画案　The external appearance project of R restaurant

7. Oショッピングモール内の食器販売コーナー　The tableware area in the O shopping mall

8. F焼き肉レストランのインテリア　Interior view of the F Korean barbecue restaurant

9. Pイタリアンレストラン計画案。オープンキッチンを見る　View of the open kitchen in the P Italian restaurant project

Particularly for women, I presume, shopping is one of the most exciting actions in our daily life. It easily and immediately refreshes our feeling. Enjoyable design for shops and shopping malls helps us with shop comfortably and makes us feel just doing window-shopping. Agreeable shop design gathers people spontaneously. I drew such pleasant views of shopping.

In works for this part in this book, I created exciting scenes of an Asian market place. It is powerful and vivid. Shops represent cultural backdrop of a country. I will be great if you feel exoticism in these drawings of scenes of eating and shopping.

10. Nデリカテッセンのエントランスから見た全景　Whole view of the N delicatessen from the entry

ゲームパーク＆カラオケルーム
Game Park & Karaoke Rooms

1. Hパーク・カーニバルゾーンのゲームコーナー　　The game arcade of carnival zone in the H amusement park

これらは，わざわざ休日を使わなくても，アフターファイブに楽しめる「気晴らし」感覚のアミューズメントスペースです。今回の作品は，生活のそばにあってドアを入れば異次元空間を思わせる，そういうイメージでプランしています。ゲームセンターは，店内にテーマ性をもたせて意匠にこだわってみました。店内がひとつのストーリーを醸し出す雰囲気を感じてもらえれば，また違った楽しみが持てるのではないでしょうか。また，ボウリング場は，これまでの既成の概念を打ち崩す，それ自体がひとつの大きなゲーム機であるという今までと違ったコンセプトで描いてみましたが，いかがでしょうか？

2. Sゲームパークのゾーンジョイント用通路
The corridor for connecting zones in the S game park

3. Sゲームパークのホースレースゾーン
The horse racing game zone
in the S game park

4. Sゲームパークのメーンホール計画案
The main hall project in the S game park

5. Jボウリング場のレーンとイルミネーションデザイン計画案　The bowling lane and illumination project in the J bowling alley

6. Jボウリング場・レーン正面パネルのトリックデザイン計画案　The trick design for bowling lane pannel in the J bowling alley

7. Oカラオケルームのエントランスゲート　The entrance gate of O karaoke rooms

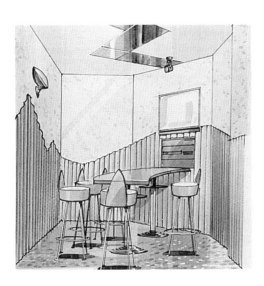

8. Oカラオケルームの個室内部デザイン
Interior view of the rooms in the O karaoke rooms

Game centers and karaoke rooms are, needless to say, very popular for us as so-called after-five-amusements in this country. Design concept of both is that once you enter the door of either places, you will feel you stepped into the another world.
I expressed each theme of each area of a game center. The interior of the project was designed to show visitors a flow of a story pleasantly. As for a project of a bowling alley, I invented revolutionary one, which is I believe epoch-making. How do you like it ?

パチンコ・パーラー
Pachinko Parlor

1. Mパチンコパーラー計画・外観夕景　The external appearance of M pachinko parlor

最近、パチンコを楽しむ客層に変化が現れ、女性客が非常に増えているといいます。それに伴って店側も、いっそうお洒落な雰囲気を重視する傾向にあります。作品にもそういったイメージを反映させています。建築的要素としては打ち放しのシンプルなものから木の温もりを感じさせるものなど、パターンはいろいろですが、以前のようなギラギラしたネオンサインはめっきり少なくなり、シンプルなもの、あるいは落ち着いたムードを重視したものに変わってきています。また、女性向けの景品を増加させたり、ある程度のレストスペースを設けることで、単にエキサイティングなゲームを楽しむ場としてだけではなく、一般的な大人向けのアミューズメントとして間口を広げていく過程での作品となりました。

2. Sパチンコパーラー計画・外観夕景　The external appearance of S pachinko parlor

3. Rパチンコパーラー計画・外観夕景　The external appearance of R pachinko parlor

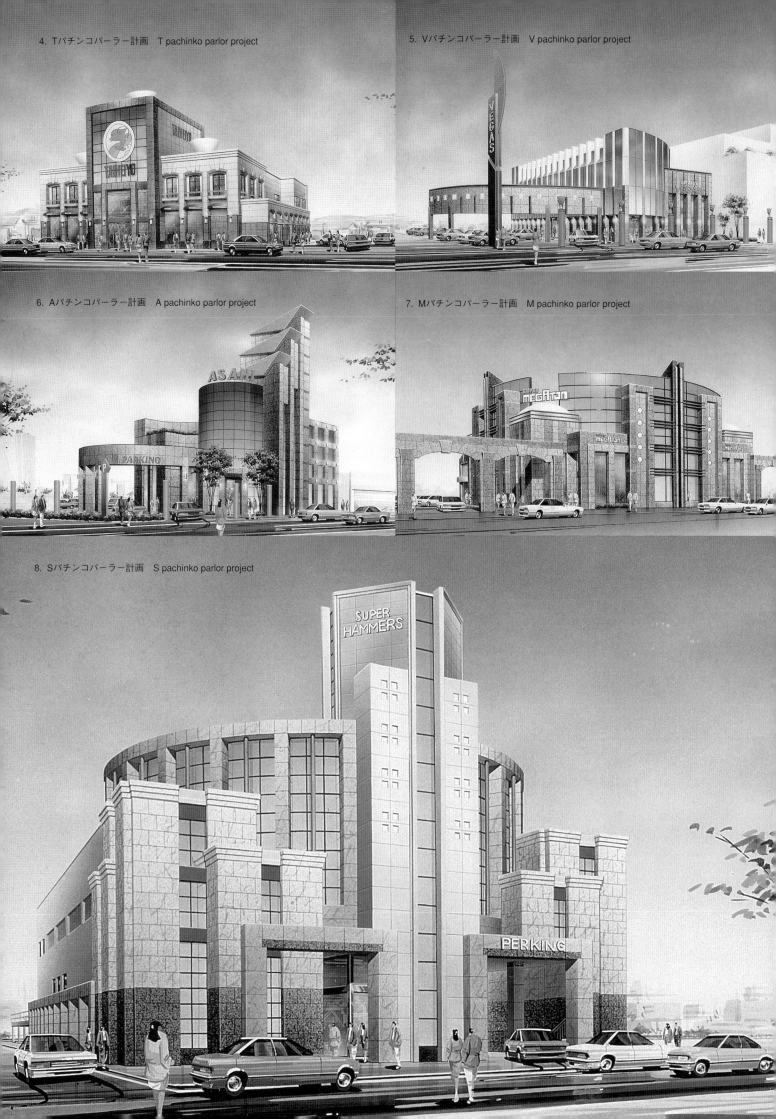

4. Tパチンコパーラー計画　T pachinko parlor project

5. Vパチンコパーラー計画　V pachinko parlor project

6. Aパチンコパーラー計画　A pachinko parlor project

7. Mパチンコパーラー計画　M pachinko parlor project

8. Sパチンコパーラー計画　S pachinko parlor project

9. Iパチンコパーラー・レストコーナー　View of the resting area in the I pachinko parlor

10. Iパチンコパーラー・スロットコーナー　View of the slot machine area in the I pachinko parlor

11. Iパチンコパーラー・景品コーナー　View of the premium goods area in the I pachinko parlor

12. Hパチンコパーラー・ペアシート＆バーコーナー
View of the pair seats and bar area in the H pachinko parlor

13. Hパチンコパーラー・ペアシート＆バーコーナー　View of the pair seats and bar area in the H pachinko parlor

In recent years, more and more women love to play pachinko, I heard. Keeping up with this trend, pachinko parlors decorate themselves fashionably. In my drawings of pachinko parlors, I considered the tendency of this industry and users. Pachinko parlors are varied from an exposed concrete high-tech one to warm-feeling wood one. Over-decorated parlors vanish gradually and simpler or chic ones prevail. Some parlors cater for women with goods and some parlors have rest lounges. New pachinko are now the places not only for fanatic gaming but also socializing as an amusement center for adults. My drawings reflect currents of the times.

第2章
制作のプロセスとノウハウ
Know-how and Process

三つのコツをマスターすればスケッチパースは描ける

Mastering Three Knacks Gives You Perspective Drawings

書店へ行けば，エンターテインメント関係の本はたくさん並んでいます。そこには，われわれの好奇心をかき立てる素晴らしい作品があり，行ってみたい，体験してみたいという気持ちにさせられます。しかしながら，これまでそのプロセスを掲載したものに出合うことがなかったのはなぜか？　これまでスケッチのプロセスなんて教えられないという思い込みが，プロセス（描き方）の本の出現を拒んでいたように思います。そこには，描き方というハードな部分と，何を描くかというソフトな部分を混同しているために，誤解が生じています。

描く内容は人それぞれの頭に浮かぶ「ひらめき」…感性のなせる技ですから，「これを描くべきだ」というような画一的なものはありません。しかし，描き方には一定のルール，あるいはコツといってもいい，それをクリアすれば，イメージスケッチは描けるというラインがあります。ここでは，このラインを習得してほしいと思います。

描けないという方の悩みは，見ただけで「こんなたいへんなものは描けない」と思い込んでしまい，おそらく，"スケッチを描く＝面倒なこと"であると感じてしまうことに端を発しています。細かな図法なんかにこだわらずに描ければいいのにと考えるのが人間の本能でしょう。この悩みを解決するには，時間をかけずに描くコツをつかむこと，何となく立体的なもの（プロポーション）が描けるコツをつかむこと，この2点をクリアすることです。ではそのためには，どういう練習が効果的か？　一言で言えば，デッサン力を身につけること，これに尽きます。何だ，やっぱり面倒なことをしなければいけないんじゃないか，と思われるかもしれません。何も，木炭を片手に石膏像とにらめっこしろというのではありません。身近にあるものをしっかり見て，ありのままを描く練習をするということ，そしてそれを何度も繰り返し続ければよいのです。そのコツはこの章にすべて網羅されています。

コツ1.＝構図をとる

何をどう見せるか，基本となるのは全体のバランスです。全体のバランスが良ければ，だいたいのものは良く見えるものです。中心はどこに置くのか？　広がりがほしいのか？　動きがほしいのか？　静止の状態か？　曲線のやさしさがほしいのか？　直線の強さが……，これらの決め手となるのが構図です。バランスを見る力，これはすべてのデザインをしていく上でも欠かせないものです。

Know-how and Process

In bookstores, we find books and books about entertaining facilities. They contain many superb drawings of projects, which we feel like experiencing. Those books, however, hardly show us the drawing process. Why ? I guess publishers have a wrong impression that books could not teach the process of drawing. They might confuse the hard or know-how of drawing with the soft or objects of drawing. Although a sense and inspiration show us what to draw, we cannot find standard rules about it. None the less, we know some basic guide lines that we should learn. I hope readers will acquire them by reading this book.

Good model drawings intimidate anybody who has difficulty in drawning, for he is apt to think that he cannot draw such splendid ones and feel that drawing is troublesome work. Many people are likely to draw their own way, being free from drawing method. To avoid this easy way, we must learn knacks to draw in short time and to get proportion of three dimensional objects.

Just learn both knacks.

Then, what should we do to learn more ? It is nothing but developing skills of sketching. You may think it will be a bother. I do not recommend you to just keep fixing your eyes on a plaster statue with fusain in your hand. All you have to do is, I think, to observe things around you carefully to draw them as they are. You have only to repeat it. Knacks are following.

Knack 1 Composition

You must consider the total balance of the composition when you think what and how to draw. The composition fundamentally defines a drawing. It decides the central point, span, movement, static/dynamic feeling, soft/hard lines, etc. You must have a sense of balance when you draw.

Knack 2 Viewing Point

Another essential element of a drawing is setting viewing (station) point or eye position. How do you look at an object ? You look it up or look it down ? You look

コツ2.＝目線（視線）

さらに構図に必要なのが目線です。上から見るか，下から見るか，横から，それとも斜めから……。見せたいものを効果的に見せる方法を追求するにはこの目線は重要です。全体を見渡すなら上から見下ろすように，大きく迫力をつけるのであれば下から見上げる，一部分をしっかりとらえるなら横から，アン・シンメトリーな状態で動きをつけるなら斜めから，それぞれのスケッチに合ったアングルがとれるようになればしめたものです。

コツ3.＝ポイントをつける

全体のバランスがとれたら，絵の仕上げは添景物の描き込みです。人，植栽，車等，描く時の注意事項は基本的なサイズの把握です。これが狂うと全体のスケール感が大きく変わりますから気をつけてください。また，絵全体のインパクト，雰囲気をいちばん出しやすいポイントがこの添景物です（添景物の応用については第3章に譲ります）。この章をじっくり読み進み，手順を踏んで描く練習を繰り返すことで必ず描けるようになります。

さらに，効果的に描く要素のひとつに，画材の選択があります。重厚感を与えるならポスターカラーが，シャープなものならエアブラシが適切でしょう。ただ，これらはかなりの作業時間を必要とします。そういう意味では，手軽なマーカーや色鉛筆も簡単な色づけには有効な画材です。しかし，われわれがお勧めするのは，淡彩―透明水彩による着彩です。この描法であれば短時間で仕上がりますし，さらに優しい表現からタッチをつけることによって勢いもつけられます。15色程度の絵の具を混ぜ合わせることによって何万色もの色を作り出すこともできます。もちろん，どうしても時間のないときは陰影だけを施した無彩色の仕上げも可能です。

最近では，この分野へのコンピューターの進出も目覚ましいものがあります。スケッチの場合も，おおまかなボリュームを入力し，アングルを決定しておけば非常に合理的です。しかしながら，コンピューターは数値入力による表現方法なので，「いい加減」で「適当」に「こんな感じ」という曖昧さは持ち併せていません。そこは人間の手で描き込み，仕上げていくことになります。曖昧さは人間のもつ優れた感覚であり，白黒を問わず，"ちょうどいい加減"を表現することを可能にします。イメージスケッチにおけるちょうどいい加減こそが，これから挑戦するスケッチの醍醐味と言えるでしょう。

at it directly or diagonally ? Viewing point is very important to express the object impressively. To show the whole object, you will look over it. To show it dynamically, you will look it up. To emphasize a part of the object, you will put your eye position aside. To make a scene asymmetric and active, you will put your viewing point far from the center line of vision and the object. When you understand the effect of moving the viewing point, you will be able to get the right viewing point easily.

Knack 3

After you decide the composition, you will add figures, plants, trees, vehicles, and so on to enhance the overall effect of a drawing. The basic point here is to use the right scale. Objects to a wrong scale make the whole drawing imbalance.

Added objects are accents of the drawing and they create an atmosphere. (See Chapter Three). Reading this chapter carefully and doing exercise repeatedly step by step, you will be surely able to draw nicely.

Selecting drawing material is also important. Poster color is good for expressing heaviness and air-brush for sharpness. Both need much time. Markers and color pencils work quickly. I recommend clear water color. It performs speedily, makes either soft or hard touch, and produces more than ten thousand colors, mixing only fifteen colors. If you have short time to work, you can draw a mono-tone drawing by water color, just putting shadow and shade on it.

Today, computers help to draw amazingly. If you input rough data of volume and station point into your computer, you will get a neat and accurate drawing. However, computer drawing is mechanically based upon digital data, so it cannot express nuances or delicate touch and feeling. We have to add something to retouch drawings after all. Ambiguity is very human idea and expression, which excludes black-or-white dichotomy and enables us to use optimum expression in nuance. The most challenging thing about drawing is how you use such nuances.

スケッチパースを描く前に
Before You Draw

描く対象物やその場面をイメージしてみましょう。手前に飛び出すジェットコースターや波にのまれる船のように迫力のあるものなのか，どっしりとした重厚感のある建物か，あるいはお花畑の中のハイキングのような優しい風景なのか……。そのイメージによって最も効果的な構図を決定します。

『構図』

1. どっしりとした安定感のあるもの
シンボリックにする場合は全体が左右対称になるように意識し，画面の中心より上の部分に高い頂点がくる二等辺三角形を感じさせることができるとよいでしょう。画面の中央，下の部分に重心を置くのがコツです。

2. 迫力や動きのほしいもの
画面の左右どちらかの一番強調したい部分に重心を置き，それとバランスが取れるように，他を配置するとよいでしょう。
＊2の動きを小さくすれば，落ち着いた表現が可能です。

目線と消点

HL＝ホリゾントライン（目線）
水平線のこと。パースやスケッチでは，目の高さを表し，画面上の垂線に対して左から右に垂直に交わる線のことです。

VP＝バニシングポイント（消点／消失点）

幾何学上，平行線同士は絶対交わることがないとされています。しかし，線路や長く続く並木道が遠くで一点に交わって見えた経験はありませんか？理論上は交わるはずのない平行線が交わっている，この点を消点（消失点）と呼んでいます。スケッチでは，左記の2つをたよりに描きはじめます。HL（水平線）というのは，画面上のどの位置に立って見ても同じはずですから，任意に立つ位置を決定してHLまで垂線を引けば，すべて同じ高さを示します。また，すべての奥行きを形づくる線はVP（消点）に集まります。

HL＝1,000mmとして描いています。

1. 底面が地面に接した立方体（1辺＝600mm）を描く／1消点
任意の点からHLに引いた垂線の5分の3が高さ600mm。それを一辺とする正方形を描き，各頂点をVPに結びます。側面にできた三角形を正方形に見える位置で切り取ります。

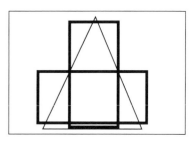

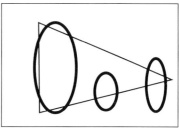

『構図　Composition』

2. 底面が地面から800mm浮いた立方体（1辺＝600mm）を3つ並べて描く／2消点
任意の点からHLを突き抜けて引いた垂線の5分の4が800mm。その位置から上に高さ600mmを取り，VP2,3に結びます。高さ600mmを2等分すれば300mm。これもVP3に結び，立方体の中央を走る線を描いてください。さらにVP3方向の奥行きを取るために立方体の対角線を利用して600mmの立方体を3つ並べます。VP2方向の正方形は目分量で切り取ります。

Imagine what you draw and how you look at it. Your object is a speeding roller coaster? A ship sinking in the sea ? A grandiose building ? Or a view of a hiking in a flower field ? Remember composition of your drawing depends on what you draw.

Composition

1.To draw a massive object, symmetric composition makes it more monumental. Use isosceles triangle composition whose top is in the top portion of a drawing. It is important to locate a station point near the bottom of the picture and the center of the drawing.

2.To draw a dynamic object, locate viewing point close to the object on either right or left side to the object. Then, draw other related details, keeping good balance with it.
＊You can get a rather static view of the object, when you locate the viewing point near the center line of vision.

Viewing Point and Vanishing Point
HL (Horizon Line)
HL shows the height of the eye level. It extends a straight horizontal line parallel to the ground.
Vanishing Point (VP)
In Euclidian geometry, parallel lines never intersect. But, we know from our experience, that any two or more parallel lines appear to converge and meet at a point. Remember landscapes of railroad and a tree-lined street. This point is called the vanishing point. On your perspective drawing, you should start to set two essential points mentioned above. Horizon line will appear same from any position. Any sight lines to create depth vanish to the same vanishing point.

In this drawing, HL=1,000mm.

1. Draw a cube whose side is 600mm on the ground on a one point perspective.

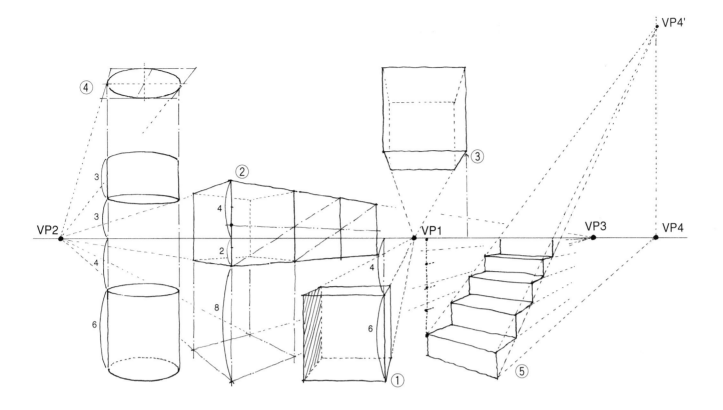

3. 底面が地面から1,600mm浮いた立方体
（1辺＝600mm）／1消点
1を参照
1はHLよりも低い位置にあるので上面が
見えます。
2はHLに重なっているので上面も下面も
見えません。
3はHLよりも高い位置にあるので下面が
見えます。

4. 底面が地面に接した円柱，地面から
1,300mm浮いた円柱（直径600mm，高さ

600mm）を描く／1消点
まず，その円柱の円の面が外接する正方
形をHLから距離を置いた位置にとり，そ
の中に円を描き，正確な高さに移動させ
ます。このときHLの近くだと，円が歪ん
でしまうので注意してください。正確な
円の面の高さが決まったら，上の面と下
の面を結んで円柱を完成させます。

5. 地面から1,000mmの高さまで5段階で
登る階段（2消点）
登り始めの位置を任意に求め，HLに向け

て垂直を引きます。その線を5等分して
蹴上げの高さを求め，VP4へ結びます。
一段目の踏面の奥行きを決め2段目の蹴
上げとの交点と登り始めの接地面と結
び，上に向けて延長します。その延長線
が，VP4から上に延ばした垂線と交わっ
たところをVP4´とし，階段勾配の角度
を決定する時，使用します。手前側面が
形づくれたら，VP2に結び正面側の階段
に幅を取って完成です。

Locate a point on the horizon line, then draw a vertical line below. Divide the line three to five. Draw lines from apexes to the VP1.

2. On a two point perspective, draw three cubes 800mm above the ground level.
Locate a point somewhere far below the HL and extend it vertically over the HL. 4/5 of the line shows 800mm. From there draw a 600mm line upward and connect it to VP2 and VP3. Divide the line by two, and you get 300mm line. Draw a line from there to the VP3. Draw a line going through the center of cubes and lines from each top of cubes to VP3. To create depth, make three cubes drawing diagonal

lines. Length of sides of cubes (VP2 side) are measured by eye.

3. 1,600mm above the ground level, draw a cube whose side is 600mm. One point perspective (VP1). See 1.
Top plane of cube 1 shows, as it is under HL.
Top and bottom planes of cube 2 do not show, as they are over HL.
Bottom plane of cube 3 shows, as it is over HL.

4. Draw cylinders (diameter 600mm and height 600mm each). One is on the ground and another is 1,300mm above the ground. One point perspective.

5. Draw 1,000mm high stairs on a two point perspective. Set a point and extend it vertically towards HL. Divide the line to five equal segments to get the rises of the stairs. Draw lines form each point to the VP4. Decide the length of run of the first stair. Draw a line from the intersection point of the first run and the second rise to the starting point on the ground. Then, extend the line upward far above the HL and link it to an extended vertical line form VP4. Here we get VP4´ with which we can get slope or angle of the stairs. After you draw the triangle sides of the stairs, you draw width, treads, and rise of the stairs.

街並みを描く
One Point Perspective of a Street

通りの下描き（HL＝1.5m，道幅：7.5m，建物：高さ1階3m＋2階3m＝6m，間口は約6m）

1.

2階建てのヨーロッパ風の家が続く街並みです。道は遠くの方で左に折れ曲がります。ここが見せ場になります。

地面上，任意の点AよりHLに向けて垂線を引きます。HLまでが1.5mであることを利用して間口方向に5倍すると7.5mの道幅が取れます。次に階高を取ります。点Aより上に垂線を引き，HL1.5mをたよりに3m（点B），6mの高さを取ります。点Aと点BとVP1を結び，できた三角形の中に，ABを一辺とする正方形を目分量でとります（斜線部分）。その正方形を2等分するかたちでHLが通っているので，これ

を利用して奥行き方向の寸法を3mで割り付け，建物の間口6mをとってゆきます。道が左に折れ曲がる部分から奥については，VP2を使って寸法を取ります。

2.

屋根，窓，入り口等のデザインをしながら描き込んでゆきます。屋根の棟ラインはVP1を使って描いている時は水平ですが，VP2を使用した棟ラインはまた異なるVPとなります。

3.

窓や屋根のディテールの描き込みや照明ポール(高さ＝3.5m)，フラッグや人を描き込みます。その場合，HLやVPを使用して同じ高さのものは揃うように注意してください。

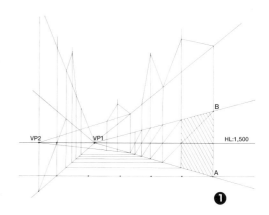

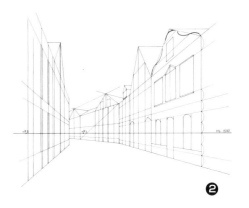

HL:1,500mm high, road:width 7,500mm, house: 1st fl. 3,000mm high, 2nd fl. 3,000mm high, frontage 6,000mm wide)

1. European two-story houses along a street. The street curves to the left, which gives you a chance to show your skill on this drawing.
Locate point A on the right and draw a vertical line to HL. This line shows 1,500mm.
Draw horizontal line from Point A to the left, and you get width of the street (1,500mm × 5 = 7,500mm). Draw a vertical line from point A up to 3,000mm. This is point B. Connect point A, B, and VP1 one another. In the triangle (ABVP1), draw a square, measuring by eye. One side of the square is AB. (See the shaded portion in the drawing). HL divides the square by two equal segments. Draw diagonal lines inside the square from point B. Draw vertical lines from the intersections of the diagonal lines and vertical lines extended from line AVP1. Dividing line AVP1 by diagonal lines, 3,000mm by 3,000mm, you get 6,000mm frontage for each houses. Curving portion is drawn by using VP2.

2. Draw roofs, windows, doors, etc. In one point perspective, lines of roofs are parallel to the horizon line but in two point perspective they are different.

3. Draw details such as lamp balls (3,500mm h) and banners. Consider the heights of same things in perspective.

人物を描く
Figures Walking and Standing

1. 立位の人　HL = 1,500

人の目の高さは，HL1,500mmの高さに合わせて楕円で型取り，その中に鼻と口と目のラインを縦，横に入れて表します。顔，胴体，手足を大まかな形で捉えます。男性は女性よりも少し高めに描き，子供は大人の身長を目安に半分くらいの位置に頭を描きます。

手前に見えてくる人は，服装などもある程度描き込みます。遠くにいる人は，あまり描き込まず，人だと認識できる程度に表現しておきます。

2. 座っている人　HL = 1,200

HL1,200mmくらいのところが，座っている人の目になるように描きます。HL上に顔を楕円で取り，椅子の座面を400mm程度で取り，そこまでを胴体として描きます。

3. その他の動きのある人

（自転車に乗っている人）HL = 1,500
顔の顎のあたりが，HL1,500mmにくるように頭の形を取ります。車輪の高さを600〜700mmくらいに取り，自転車のボリュームを取ってから，サドルと顔までの間に胴体を入れ，少し前かがみになるように描くと自転車に乗っている感じが描けます。

（走っている人）HL = 1,500
左手が前の時は左足は後ろに残し，手足を交互にして体の重心を少し前ぎみにして描くと走っている様子が描けます。

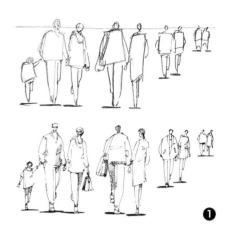

1. Figures Walking and Standing.
HL=1,500mm.

Firstly, draw sketchy ovals for figures, considering that their eye level is 1,500mm. Add some lines to show their noses, mouths, and eyes. Draw roughly their faces, bodies, and limbs. Men are a little bit taller than women. Adults are two times higher than children. Figures at short distance need details but not small ones. Distance make shapes of small figures vague.

2. Sitting Figures. HL=1,200mm

HL goes over eyes of sitting figures in this drawing. Draw an oval to make a head of the man. Suppose the height of a chair is 400mm, and draw each body of figures on chairs.

3. Active Figures Cyclist. HL=1,500mm

Draw a head with HL on his chin. The height of the tire is 600~700mm. Draw roughly the bicycle and body with a slouch.
Runner (HL=1,500mm)
He moves his arms and feet by turns and runs with a little slouch.

自動車と庭を描く
Automobiles and Gardening Objects

1. 自動車
HL＝1,500

HL1,500mmを目安に，タイヤの接地面を決めます。通常，車のルーフの高さは1,2000mmくらいですから，接地面からHL1,500mmまでの距離の4／5の位置にその高さが取れます。それぞれの車のパーツの面積の比率や位置の割合を，見本で確認しながら車の形を大まかに捕えます。4輪駆動やワンボックスの大型車の場合は，ルーフの位置が1,700mmくらいなので，HLをたよりに最高高さを割り出します。タイヤの位置やガラス面，フロントグリルのプロポーションに注意して全体の形を整えてゆきます。

2. ガーデニング
HL＝1,200

テーブルの天板の高さ（約700mm）を，地面からHL1,200mmの半分より少し上に取ります。その高さをたよりにテーブル全体のプロポーションを決めてゆきます。イスの場合は座面の高さが400mmくらいなので，地面からHLまでの距離の1／3を目安にします。背もたれは700～800mmくらいの高さとして，HLまでの距離の2／3を目安にして椅子の形を整えます。

❶
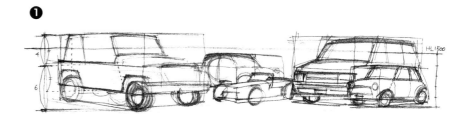

❷

1. Automobile
HL=1,500mm

Roof top is usually 1,200mm high. Referring to sample photos, understand the position and proportion of car parts, and draw them correctly. Roof height of four-wheel-drive cars, wagons, vans, and other big cars is 1,700mm. Notice position of tires, proportion of windows and grills.

2. Gardening Objects
HL=1,200mm

Height of a table is 700mm. Table top is little bit above the middle between HL and the ground level. Upon the height, decide the proportion of the table. Seating height of chairs is 400mm. The back of the seat in 700~800mm high.

樹木を描く
Plants

1. 高木
（左からケヤキ，マツ，ワシントンパーム，
ポプラ，クスノキ）HL＝1,500

それぞれ，樹木の高さはHLを目安に描き
ます。たとえば，ケヤキは通常6m以上
はありますので，HLの4倍ということに
なります。

また樹形はその樹木の特徴を表現する大
切な部分です。それぞれの特徴をうまく
つかんで描きましょう。

ケヤキ／上に広がる扇形　マツ／上に伸
びる三角形　ワシントンパーム／高さの
1／3くらいの箇所に葉を密集させる　ポ
プラ／細長く下の部分に膨らみをもたせ，
風になびくイメージで　クスノキ／全体
に入道雲のようにモコモコと丸い表現を

2．中低木
（左からウメ，ツツジ，モミジ，ジンチョ
ウゲ，ユキヤナギ，アジサイ）HL＝1,000

1. From the left, zelkova, pine, Washington
palm, poplar, and camphor tree. HL=1,500mm.
Height of tree are decided upon the HL.
Zelkova, for example, is usually over 6,000mm,
so it is four times higher than the HL. Express
each characteristics of trees, thinking shapes of
the trees.

2. Zelkova is like a fan and pine an acute
triangle. Draw leaves of a Washington palm
trees on top most segment. Poplar is slender
and its lower part smells and often bends in
the wind. A camphor looks like a thunderhead.

アミューズメントパーク
Process of Drawing an Amusement Facility

通常，目にすることのできない工事現場をモチーフにしたアミューズメントパークのスケッチパースです。骨組みだけの建物や，足場を利用したジェットコースター，特殊工作機のデザイン遊具，破れた鉄管の噴水など，日常そばにあっても近寄れない，好奇心をそそるアミューズメントを再現しています。

使用用具
線画：インキング／フエルトペン
紙質：コピー用普通紙（タックボード貼り）
着彩：透明水彩着彩

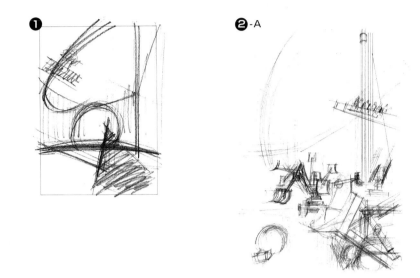

❶　　❷-A

1. 構図の決定

遠くまで見渡せる，広がりのあるスケッチにするために，HL＝3,000mmに設定しています。迫力のあるハンギングコースターを左手に，手前右下にブルドーザー，その上にH形鉄骨のバイキング。その向こうには杭打ちのジャイアントドロップ，中央にパワーショベルのオクトパス。バックは，遠景に取り囲んだ鉄骨組みの建物。迫力と重量感と荒々しさの中に楽しさを出せるような構図にしています。

2. 下描き

1で取った構図の垂直線の補正を加えながら，乗り物に人物を入れてゆき，よりスケール感をはっきりさせます。

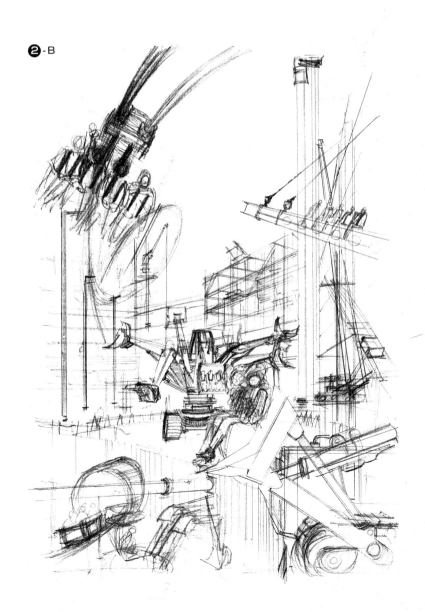

❷-B

3. マーカー着彩

ラフスケッチの状態でコピーを取り，マーカーで色彩計画を行います。簡単なプレゼンテーションの場合はこの状態で提出してもよいでしょう。マーカーは使いやすい道具ですが，色数が限られているため，画面上で色の塗り重ねをすることで近い色を作ってゆきます。手前の方にポイントとなる色を置き，遠くにゆくほどボカした感じで表現し，遠近感を醸し出します。

4. インキング

ラフスケッチを下敷きにして，上にコピー用普通紙を重ね，フエルトペンでフリーハンドのインキングを仕上げてゆきます。このとき，手前から順に描いていくことを忘れないでください。遠くの部分から描いてしまうと，本来は見えない線まで描き込んでしまう場合があります。また，手前の部分は細かいディテールの表現も要求されますので，しっかり資料を準備しましょう。

5. 背景の着彩

バックの建物に透明水彩（グレーに近い色）でさっとタッチを付けます。そのときはあまり細かいところを描かないようにしてください。光と影を表現することを心がけ，遠いところなのでコントラストをはっきり付けないように，遠くのぼやけた雰囲気を意識して描いてください。

6. 地面の着彩

イエローグレーで土の色を表現します。距離感を表現するために手前の方を少し濃く塗っておきます。

7. 遊具の着彩

遊具の中でも，まず赤から黄系統を着彩してゆきます。色を塗り重ねてゆけば，それぞれの面のコントラストを強くすることができます。

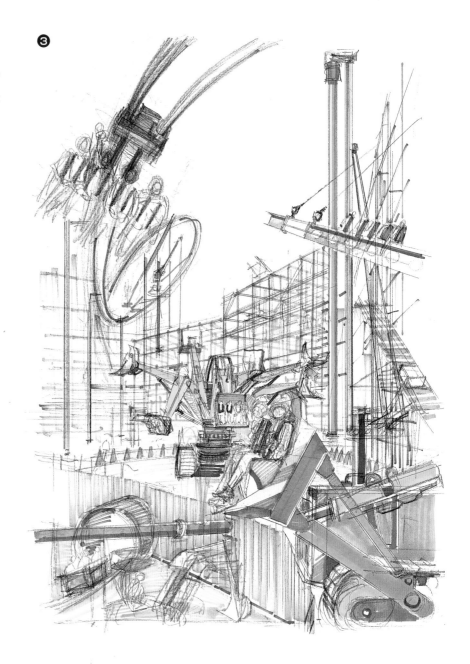

❸

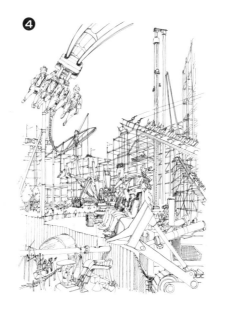

❹

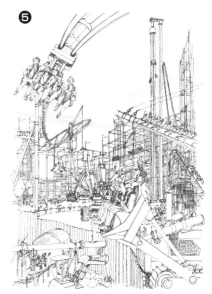

❺

An unusual drawing of an amusement facility upon construction site. Skeleton of a building, roller coaster on scaffold, amusement of heavy vehicles, a fountain of broken pipes. There are common but curious things in this facility.

Materials
Line drawing/Felt tip pens
Paper/Copied paper (tacked on a board)
Color/Clear water color

1. Composition
An extensive view with HL=3,000mm. A dynamic hanging roller coasters on the left and a bulldozer on the right, a so-called Viking vehicle (H section steel) is on top right. Over there are a giant drop (huge piling machine) and an octopus (hydraulic shovel). Background is steel construction of buildings. Composition of this drawing expresses force, massiveness, and power.

2. Sketch
Redraw vertical lines and draw figures. Notice the scale.

3. Coloring by Markers
Copy the rough drawing and color it by markers. You can use this drawing for presentation. It is easy to use marker, but the colors of markers are limited. You must make colors you need while drawing. Apply shade the drawing. The closer is the deeper and the farther is the thinner.

4. Inking
Put a sheet of copied paper on the rough drawing and draw lines by a felt-tip pen.
Draw first the bottom portion of the drawing. If you do first the top portion of the drawing, you will likely overdo. Objects at short distance need details, so you have to prepare photos and drawings you consult.

5. Coloring the Background
Use grayish colors to the background and draw lightly. You need not to draw picky details. Produce fine effect of light and shade. Do not make very strong contrast. Express the vague of the far objects at distance.

6. Coloring the Ground
Use yellowish gray to the ground. Remember the effect of shading to show distance.

7. Coloring Facilities
Use red first, then yellowish colors. Put the colors over and over, and you will show contrast as you like.

❻

❼

8. 全体の着彩
その他の遊具，まわりの建物の鉄骨部分など
を，メーンの部分を考慮しながら着彩します。

9. 仕上げ
人物，植栽，旗，水，などを描き込み，全体
の着彩の後，バランスを見てハイライトを入
れると効果的に立体感を表現できるでしょう。

8. Final Coloring
Considering colors and shapes of the major elements
(e.g. amusement facilities, steel, etc.) of the drawing,
color the rest.

9. Finish
Draw figures, plants, banners, water, etc. Put the
high light to keep harmony with the total balance as
whole to give a feeling to show volume.

スタジオ番組

Process of Drawing a Studio

子供向けのキャラクターを使用したスタジオ風景のスケッチパースです。

背景に海賊船やキャラクターのぬいぐるみ、中央に司会進行役、手前にカメラスタッフ等々がスタンバイしている状態です。鉛筆のラフ描きの上に淡彩仕上げをしています。

使用用具
線画：鉛筆スケッチ仕上げ／黒の鉛筆
紙質：コピー用普通紙（タックボード貼り）
着彩：透明水彩

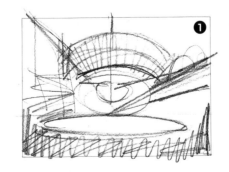

1. 構図の決定

これからアクションが始まる前兆のわくわくした感覚を表現するために、ポイントが中央にくるようにし、全体をシンメトリーに配置しておきます。

2. 鉛筆による線画

簡略した下描きの上から鉛筆で清書をし，影を鉛筆でタッチを付けながら入れてゆきます。手前のスタッフなどはスポットライトが当たらない暗い部分なので，影を落として表現します。

3. 背景と手前の着彩

後方の船，サイン，手前の影になるスタッフを着彩してゆきます。暖色は，相対的に目にやさしく，気になりにくいので，赤系統，茶系統，黄系統の箇所を続けて着彩してゆきます。

4. 緑系，青系，紫系の着彩

寒色は目に鮮やかな印象のため，これを着彩することにより，全体に色相によるメリハリを付けてゆきます。

5. 全体の着彩

全体にある程度，色が入ったら，バランスを整えるために色の濃い部分を重ね塗りして，立体感をはっきりさせてゆきます。

6. サイン等の着彩

アミューズメントの場合，サインは目立つように塗った方が，ドラマチックな雰囲気が強調され，より効果的と言えます。

7. 仕上げ

物の形状が複雑で分かりにくい部分は，コントラストを付けて立体感をだしてゆきます。また，特に光の当たる箇所にはハイライトを入れて，さらにメリハリを強調します。

❷

❸

❹

Drawing a T.V. studio scene of a kid's program in which characters play around. There are a pirate ship and characters in the background, a personalities in the center, and cameramen far off the center. Color a pencil drawing.

Material
Line drawing/Black pencil
Paper/Copied paper (on a board)
Color/Clear water color

1. Composition
Choose symmetric composition to focus on the center part of a drawing. Express exciting feeling before the program start.

2. Line Drawing by Pencil
Draw a sketch by lines. Shade it by pencil. Front figures are in the dark.

3. Coloring the Background and the T.V.Crew
Color the ship, sign, and the crew. Warm colors are soft. Use colors in order of red, brown, and yellow.

4. Green, Blue, and Purple
Cold color is striking and used to control the tone of the drawing by its hue.

5. Coloring the Rest
Redraw to emphasize some dark colored parts of the drawing. Apply a three-dimensional effect.

6. Coloring Signs
Signs should be showy and dramatic in the drawing of an amusement facility.

7. Finish
Objects in complicated shapes are drawn making a contrast with other parts of the drawing. Put some high lights to bright parts. Express dimensional feeling clearly.

❺

❻

❼

ゲームパーク
Process of Drawing a Game Park

宇宙船をテーマにしたゲームパークの中
央部分のスケッチパースです。暗い部屋
の中で光が飛び交っている雰囲気を醸し
出すために、バックを暗くし、カラフル
な照明や、その照明に照らされている箇
所が浮かび上がっているように描いてい
ます。

使用用具
線画：鉛筆トレースのみ
紙質：キャンソンボード（青）
着彩：透明水彩＋ポスターカラー＋エアブラシ

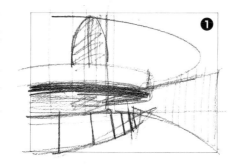

❶

1. 構図の決定
中央より左手にスペースシャトルの高い
塔があり、そのまわりに中2階部分、奥
の左手から右手前の方に2階のデッキが
円弧を描いて飛び出してくるような構図
にしています。かなりアクティブな動き
のある画面です。ビューポイントとして、
中央あたりに宇宙飛行士を置いて、全体
のバランスを取っています。

2. 下描きをする

詳細はあまり描き込まず，大まかに物の位置を確認して描いてゆきます。

3. トレースダウン

2を使って，デザインを施しながら，細かいディテールを描き込んで下絵を仕上げ，青いキャンソンボードにトレースダウンします。

4. ベースの着彩

ボードの端をマスキングして着彩範囲を決定します。青いボード上に透明水彩で垂直方向に濃淡をつけてゆきます。中2階のデッキや2階のデッキは陰になる部分ですので，暗い感じを表現します。

❷

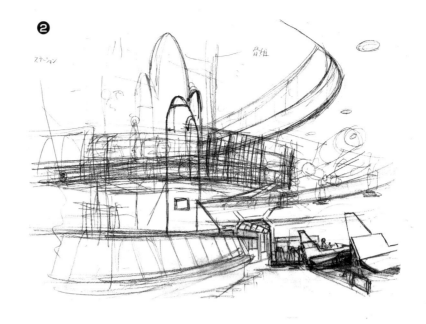

❸

Perspective of the central area of a game center park with a theme of a space ship.
To express an atmosphere of the space ship I drew flashing light in the darkness. Background is dark. Colorful lights and lit-up areas are outstanding.

Material
Line drawing/Pencils for tracing
Paper/Illustration board
Color/Clear water color+poster color+air brush

1. Composition

On the left there are space shuttle and the tower on the mezzanine. This part should appear to jump out. Active composition. Viewing point is located on an astronaut in the center, which plays a pivotal part of this composition

2. Sketch

Do not draw too many details. Consider the total composition.

3. Tracing

Design some parts of the interior and draw details. Trace the rough drawing and copied it on a blue illustration board.

4. Primary Coloring

Mask edges of the drawing. Use water color to draw shades vertically. The mezzanine and the second level are dark.

❹

⑤

⑥

5. 背景の着彩

ポスターカラーを絵の具に混ぜて，不透明な色を作り，飛行士，スペースシャトル，デッキなどの光の照明に映し出される部分を明るく，はっきりと描いてゆきます。

6. 壁面の着彩

ゲーム機の画面，宇宙ステーションなどの壁面を，薄く水で溶いたポスターカラーの絵の具を使って，垂直方向の濃淡を付けてゆきます。

7. バランスを整える

点景は照明の当たっている箇所を意識しながら描き込んでゆきます。

8. 仕上げ

エアブラシを使用して，スポットライトをはじめとする照明器具とその光を描いてゆきます。最後に全体の様子を見ながら，立体感の欲しい部分はコントラストを付け，光に映し出される部分には白のハイライトを入れて，はっきりしたスケッチになるように心がけます。

5. Coloring the Background

Mix poster color with water color to make opaque colors. Color an astronaut, space shuttle, deck, and other bright parts.

6. Coloring Walls

Use thin water color to draw fronts of game machine and walls of space station. Shade them vertically.

7. Think the Balance

Draw details, considering lit-up sides of objects.

8. Finish

Use air brush to draw spot light and other lighting. Apply three-dimensional effect to something flat. White high light on bright and shiny sides to make a clear picture.

和菓子店と洋菓子店
Process of Drawing a Confectioneries

集合店舗の一角にある，通路に面した和菓子，洋菓子の物販店を取り上げてみました。間口の広いテナントを左右の2方向からとらえたアングルで，ひとつの画面にレイアウトしました。

（使用用具）
線画：インキング　フエルトペン
紙質：コピー用紙（タックボード貼り）
着彩：透明水彩

1. 構図の決定
見せたいアングルで下描きを起こしてゆきます。今回は2方向のアングルで描いていくので別々の下描きが必要になります。

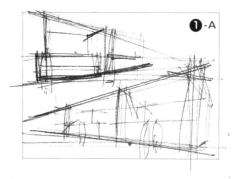

❶-A

2. インキング
インキングで注意する箇所は，ショーケースの中のケーキ，和菓子をあまり細かく描き込まないで菓子屋であることを感じさせること。人が通りがかりに覗いている，あるいは購入している，職人がお菓子作りを実演している等々，いろいろなシチュエーションをイメージし描いてゆきます。

3. 広範囲の着彩
着彩は，白っぽい石の部分→明るい木質部分→白の天井→ベージュの床という順に，広い面積で色の淡い箇所から着彩してゆきます。ガラス部分は透明感を出すために，ブルー系を中心に，白い箇所を残し

ながら帯状のグラデーションを付けてゆきます。照明の光が当たっている部分は用紙の色そのままを残して，そのまわりを着彩することで表現します。

4. 点景の着彩

人，商品，ディスプレイを着彩してゆきます。商品が決まっている場合，サンプルをよく見てしっかりと描くと，よりリアルに表現されます。人は服装の色のバランス等にも十分注意を払って下さい。手前にいる人はグラデーションや影を付けて，よりはっきりと描きましょう。

5. 仕上げ

サイン類が描き込めたら，コントラストの弱い箇所に影，ハイライトを入れ，全体をよりはっきりさせましょう。照明器具にホワイトで光っている状態を描き込んで完成です。

This is a sweet shop with wide frontage on a corner of a commercial complex. Two drawings from different viewing point on a board.

Material
Line drawing/inking by felt-tip pen
Paper/Copied paper (on a board)
Color/Water color

1. Composing

Choose direction by which you look at the shop. Two sketches.

2. Inking

Without drawing small things in a show case, you must express characteristics of the shop. Imagine various scenes of the shop where people browse and shop, and workmen make sweets, etc.

3. Coloring

In order of white stone, bright wood, white ceiling, and beige floor, you must color them. Color first wider and brighter portion of the drawing. To draw glazed part, leave blank and apply gradation on the glass. Leave shining parts and draw something around them.

4. Coloring Details

Color figures, goods, and display. If you know items of the shop, gather samples and look them carefully to draw them realistically. Notice the balance of colors used for figures. Big figures often need precise gradation and shade.

5. Finish

Put shades and high lights to dim objects and add shiny spots of objects to make whole drawing impressive.

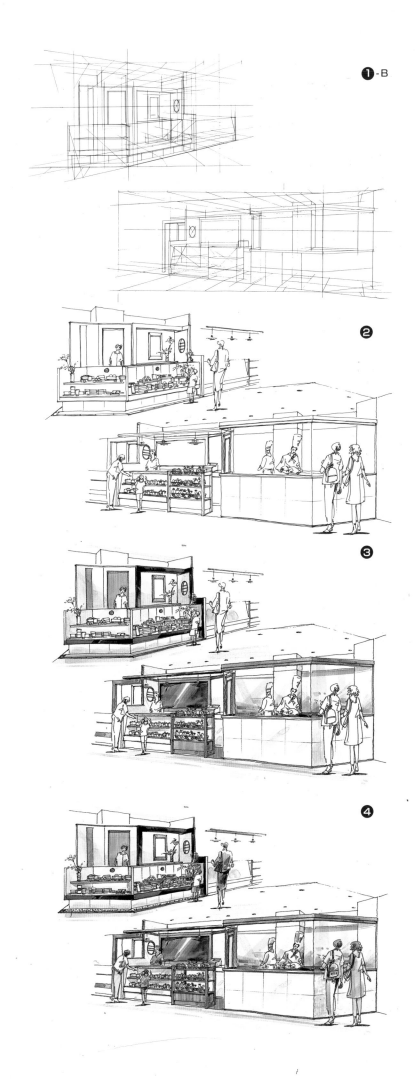

❶-B

❷

❸

❹

観光レジャー施設
Process of Drawing a Tourist Facility

街おこしを兼ねた，町の拠点となりうる
レストランや物販・展示ホール，多目的
ホールを含む庭園のある施設をここでは
取り上げました。静かな山間の町の雰囲
気と庭園の美しさを鉛筆のタッチで柔ら
かく表現しています。

使用用具
線画：鉛筆スケッチ仕上げ／黒の鉛筆
紙質：コピー用普通紙（タックボード貼り）
着彩：透明水彩

1. 下描き（CAD入力）
CADで平面データを入力します。立面に
ついては1階4m，2階3.5m，瓦屋根
葺き等のデザインを施してから入力して
ゆき，適当なアングルを探し出し出力し
ます。

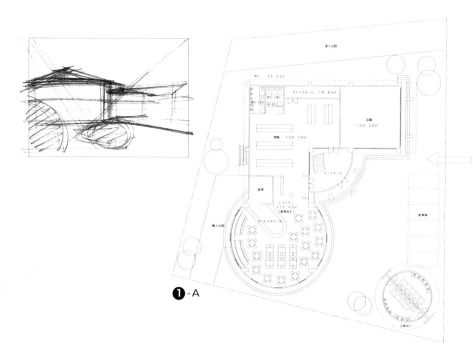

❶-A

2. ラフスケッチ

1で出力したCADデータを元に，コンピューター特有の歪みを修正し，建物の詳細なデザインを施します。庭園の雰囲気もここで描き込みます。後方の山や手前の樹木等を描き，バランスを取ってゆきます。

3. 鉛筆による線画

2のラフスケッチを下敷きに，上からコピー用普通紙をかぶせ，鉛筆で線画を仕上げます。柔らかさを出したいので，きっちりディテールを描くというよりは，全体の雰囲気を重視しながら描いてゆきます。

4. 建物のベースの着彩

画面に定着液を吹き付け，鉛筆の線で汚れないように処理した後，この線画の普通紙をタックボードに糊付けします。透明水彩で建物の屋根，壁のベースを塗ってゆきます。

❶-B

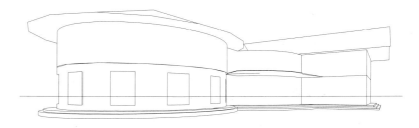

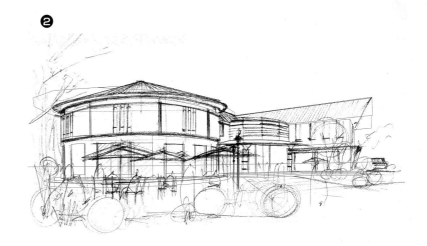

This facility is a kind of tourist information to revitalize a town. It has a shop, a hall, a gallery, and a garden. I gently drew it in a quiet environment of mountains.

Material
Line drawing/Pencil drawing
Paper/Copied paper (tacked on a board)
Color/Clear water color

1. CAD

Input data of floor plan, then elevation (the ground floor=4,000mm high, second floor =3,500mm) into computer. Choose and input your best angle and direction.

2. Sketch

Retouch distortion peculiar to computer-aided drawings. Design some part of the project on your own. Draw the garden with full details. Draw mountains in the background and trees in the garden, considering the total balance of the drawing.

3. Line Drawing by Pencil

Cover the sketch with a sheet of paper and draw lines gently. Do not be picky about details. Total feeling as whole is important.

4. Coloring Architecture

Spray fixative on the drawing to protect it from smudge. Stack it on a board. Use clear water color to draw roofs and walls.

5. 窓の着彩

1階店舗部分やレストラン部分は雰囲気を意識して黄色の明るい窓にし，2階の展示ホールは少し温かみのあるグレーで着彩します。建物内の点景や奥行き感なども意識しながらグラデーションをつけてゆきます。

6. グリーンを描く

樹木や植栽の色を黄緑色で着彩してゆきます。光の方向を意識しながら，影の部分などを塗り重ねて濃い色に仕上げてゆきます。

7. 点景の着彩

全体のバランスを見ながら，人の服装を描き込んでゆきます。派手すぎず，全体に適度な華やかさの出る配色になるように注意してください。

8. 仕上げ

ホワイトで店舗内の照明にハイライトを入れたり，植栽，空，遠景の山々等，点景や背景を全体のバランスを見ながら仕上げてゆきます。

5. Coloring Windows

Use bright colors to draw windows of the first level (shop and restaurant in there) and warm gray to the second level. Apply gradation, considering details of the interior and depth of the building.

6. Drawing Trees and Plants

Use yellowish green to draw trees and plants. Notice the light direction. Shadow must be dark.

7. Coloring Details

Color clothes of figures, studying the total balance of colored portion of the drawing. The color should be moderate not gaudy. Disperse vivid colors.

8. Finish

Put high light (white) on interior lighting. Reconsider the formation of the drawing such as plants, sky, mountains, and other details.

第3章
エンターテインメント施設のエレメント
Drawings of Entertaining Facilities

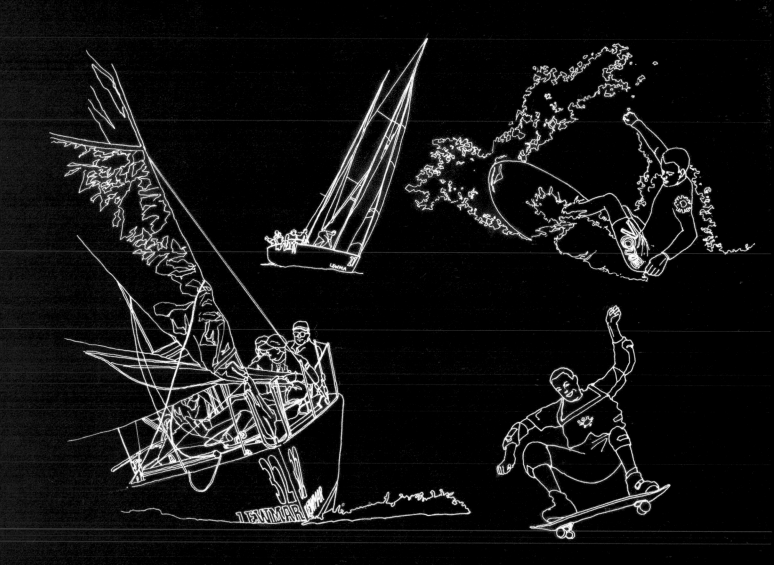

線画にしたエレメントをストックしておく
String Samples of Line Drawings

第二章でも少し触れましたが，イメージスケッチの雰囲気を伝えるポイントとして挙げられるのが添景物です。一般的なパースでは中心となる建築物やインテリアの引き立て役，いわゆる小道具的な扱いになりますが，イメージスケッチの場合，添景物が主役に匹敵する扱いをされることが多々あります。添景物というより，絵を形成するエレメンツ（パーツ）という方が，言いえているかもしれません。

エレメントの主な役割としては次のようなものが挙げられます。

1. アイキャッチとしての役割
ジャングルのイメージにおけるジープや野性動物，中世ヨーロッパ風というときの舞踏会の女性のように，全体のイメージの象徴として登場しているものがこれに当たります。もちろんこの場合，そのスケッチの中の主役に匹敵する存在であり，そのものが目立つような描き方になっています。

2. スケール感を認知させる役割
人間や車のスケールによって全体の大きさや距離感を表現することを指します。目安として人間の目線の高さは約150cm，車の高さは120cm程度と換算することができ，それを利用して全体のスケール感を無意識のうちに把握させることが可能です。また，それらが画面上で重なりあって表現されることで，遠近感を感じさせ，距離感を認識させることになります。逆に言えば，各エレメントのスケールが間違っていると絵全体のスケール感をこわすことにもなってきますので責任重大と言えます。

3. 絵の仕上げにおける役割
イメージを描いているのですから，ほとんどが曖昧なひらめきからの出発です。細かいディテールまではっきりしない場面にも遭遇します。そんな時は，描き切れない部分の前に大きな樹木や車を配置することで，そのディテールを隠してしまおうというわけです。スケッチでは，何でもかんでもしっかりと描くことは時間的な問題から考えても求められていません。雰囲気が伝わるものなら良いのです。これ

As I wrote in chapter two, figures and other additional elements are ponderable for drawings. They play small roles to show up architectures and interior design but often play grave roles in drawings. In some cases, they are not additional but crucial elements (parts) for drawings. The details have following three functions.

1. Eye-catching
Details catch eyes of seers and tell a story of a drawing instantaneously. They represent the total image of the drawing and play the main role strikingly. Typical examples are jeep and wild animals to the jungle, ladies in a ballroom of the Middle Ages in Europe.

2. Sense of Scale
Figures and trees indicate the scale of a drawing. Generally the height of the viewing point of the spectator in the drawing is 150 cm and that of a car is 120 cm. With these standards, you make viewers of a drawings get a sense of scale and distance. This type of elements give depth of the drawing together with other elements. Therefore, if you miscalculate the scale of these elements, you will break the totality of the drawing. You should be mindful of the scale of these elements.

3. Finishing
As you draw your images by intuition, you sometimes cannot get details of images. If you are in such trouble, it will be helpful to draw details to finish a

は良い意味での「ごまかしのテクニック」です。

エレメントが，このような役割を果たすことによって，何となくだったイメージはリアルさを増し，臨場感を与えられ，息づいたものになっていきます。ここで大切なのは，いかに完全なエレメントを配置するかということ。実際に「無」のものを「有」に感じさせる効果を見込んでいるのですから，エレメント自体は細かいディテールまで描けていなければなりません。この部分が粗ければ，全体の仕上がりも粗っぽく見られ，逆にしっかりと描けていれば完全なイメージを伝えることができるのです。

では，エレメントの細かいディテールを描くためにはどうすればよいのか？ これはひとつでも多くの資料に目を通し，最も適切と思われる見本を真似ることです。それではオリジナリティーがないと思わないでください。人間の記憶というのは実に頼りないもので，記憶にあるものだけで細かいディテール

まで描き込むというのは至難の技なのです。見本に忠実に描くということだけでもかなりのテクニックを要します。この場合，資料はできる限り線画になっているものの方が望ましいと言えます。なぜなら，写真等だとそれをデッサンする力がさらに要求されますが，線画になっていれば，必要最少限の線がすでに用意されているわけですから作業に無駄が少ないのです。常日頃からイメージスケッチに役立ちそうなエレメントをデッサンの練習がてら，線画にしてストックしておかれることをお勧めします。

しかし，そんな時間もないし，いったいどんなものをストックしていいのか分からないという方もいらっしゃるでしょう。そういう方のために，この章では，これまで私が描きためてきたエレメント集から代表的なものをピックアップしてみました。これを“エレメント辞典”として活用いただき，いずれはあなた独自のオリジナルの辞典ができることを願っています。

drawing. Big trees and cars conceal the unfinished images. For sketching, you do not always have to draw every single details. Expressing an atmosphere is far more important. It may be called a make-up or cosmetic technique of drawing in a positive meaning.

With a help from elements, you can get an articulate image of your object and give realistic expression and a sense of presence to your drawing. What is important here is how you draw and compose full-detailed elements. A drawing does not represent a real scene but it looks like realistic when details are well done.
If you draw an details slapdash, it will eventually break a magic of drawing reality. Rough details make the drawing rough and can not express what you intend. Wheather a drawing succeeds or not

depends on details.

How can we draw details effectively ? All you have to do is just see data and samples as many as possible and copy them. This does not mean blind imitation. As our memory is limited, we cannot draw details of something only with memory. Even copying samples needs techniques. I recommend you to use samples of line drawing, for imitating sample photos is quite hard but you can easily trace line drawings. It is desirable for you to look up sample of elements and copy them in line drawings. Some of you may say that he does not have enough time to do it. That is why I chose some of my samples drawings of elements in this chapter. I hope you will use them and make your clip art dictionary on you own in the future.

ジャングル探検シーン

The jungle expedition scenes

アフリカの動物
African animals

in .africa

鳥と昆虫
Birds and insects

家具と植物
Furniture and plants

オーシャン・シーン
Ocean scenes

海賊たちと帆船

Pirates and sailing ships

西部開拓時代
The Western frontier age

アドベンチャー・シーン
Adventure scenes

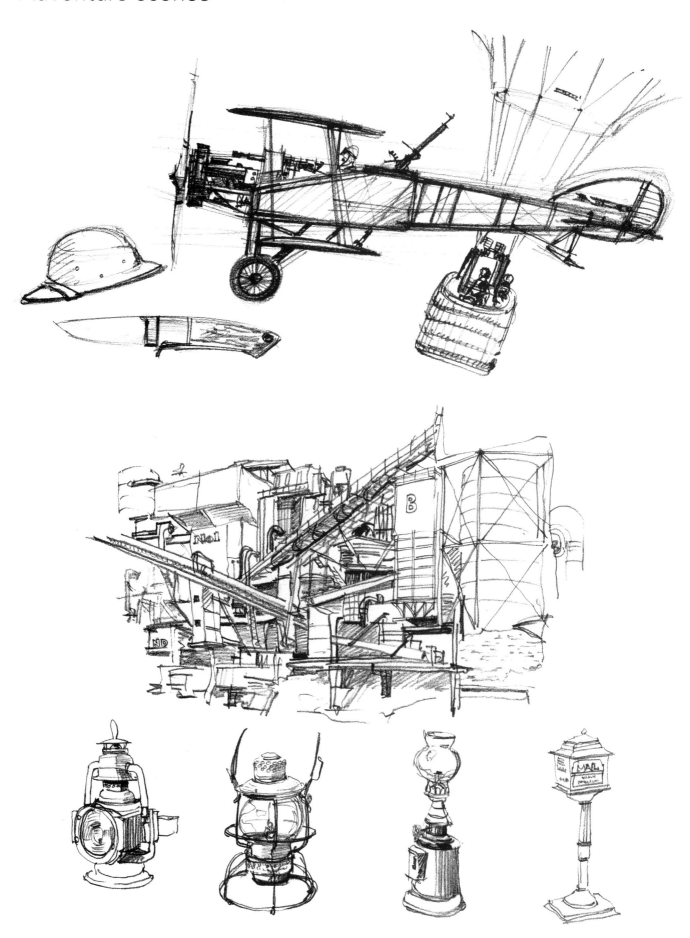

ポール＆布飾り
Poles and cloth ornaments

洞窟とトンネル
Caves and tunnels

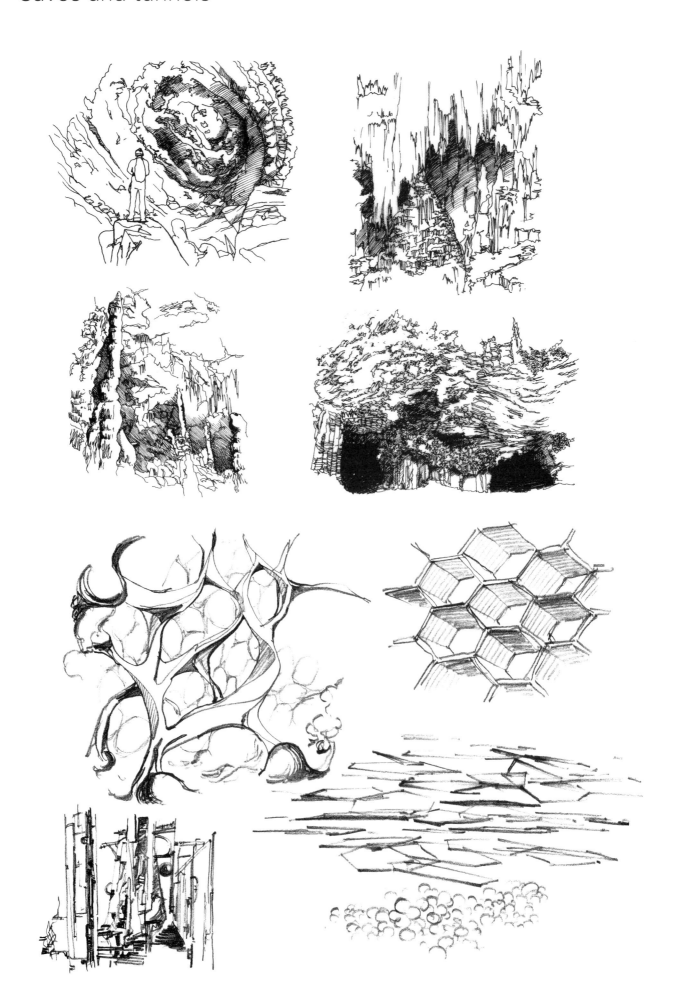

パラソルとベンチ
Parasols and benches

トロピカル・モチーフ
Tropical motif

ランプとバナー
Lamps and banners

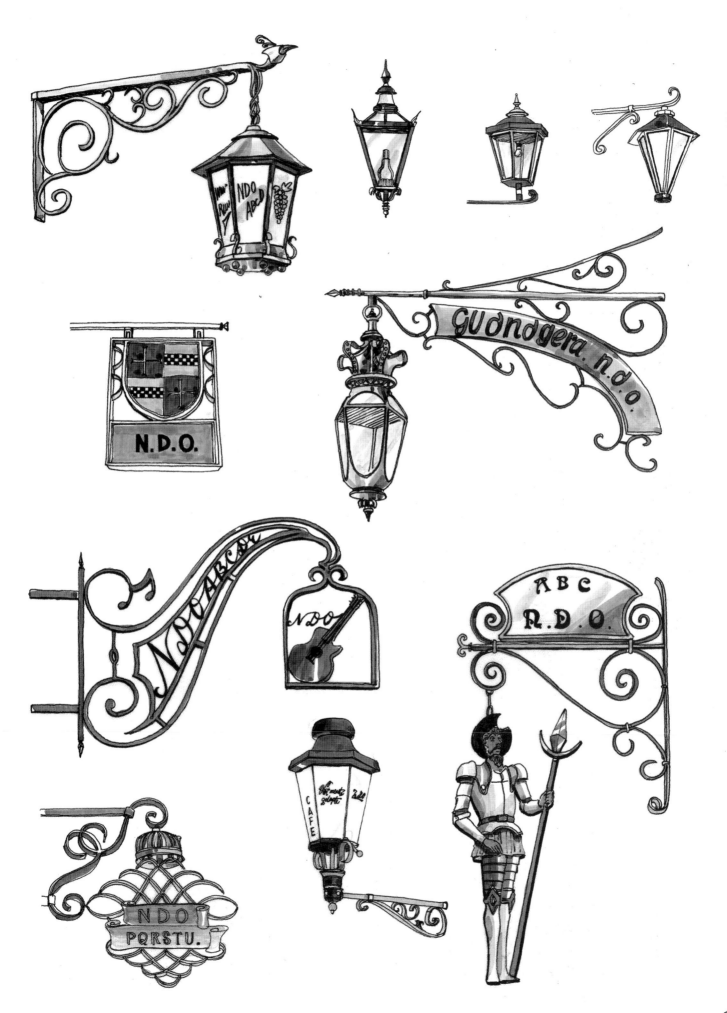

自転車とオートバイ
Bicycles and motorcycles

自動車と列車
Cars and trains

ワゴン
Wagons

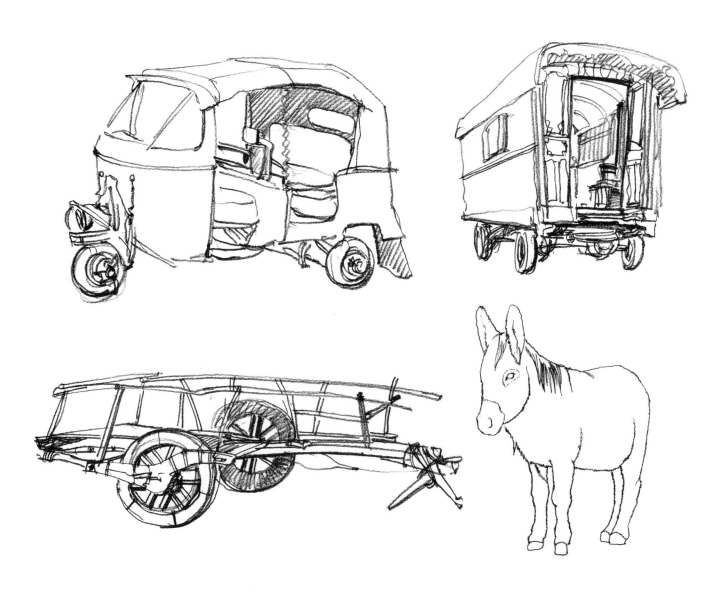

外国の民具
World folk crafts

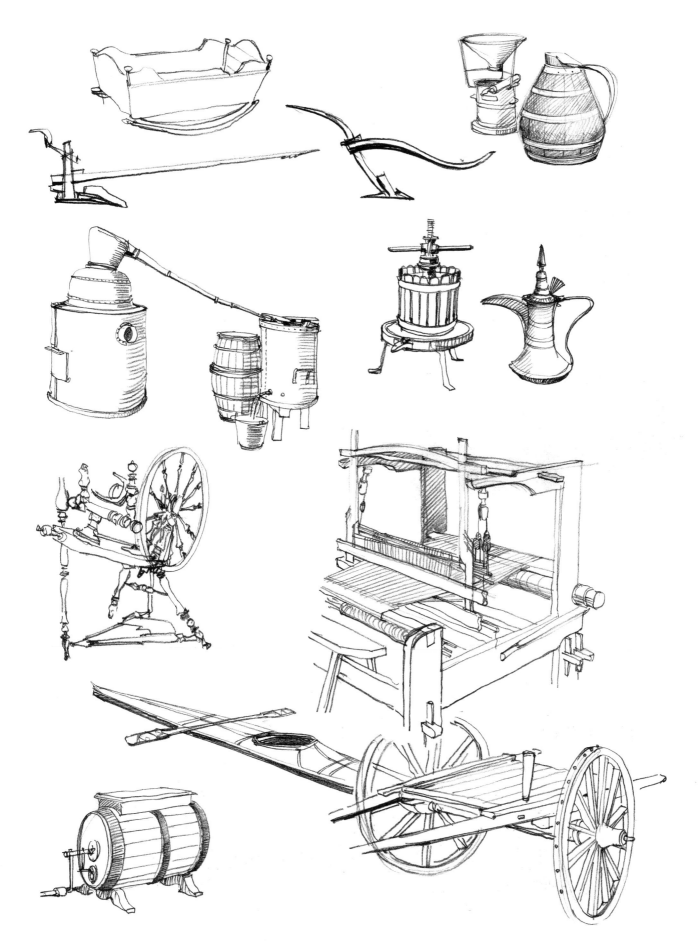

日本の民具
Japanese folk crafts

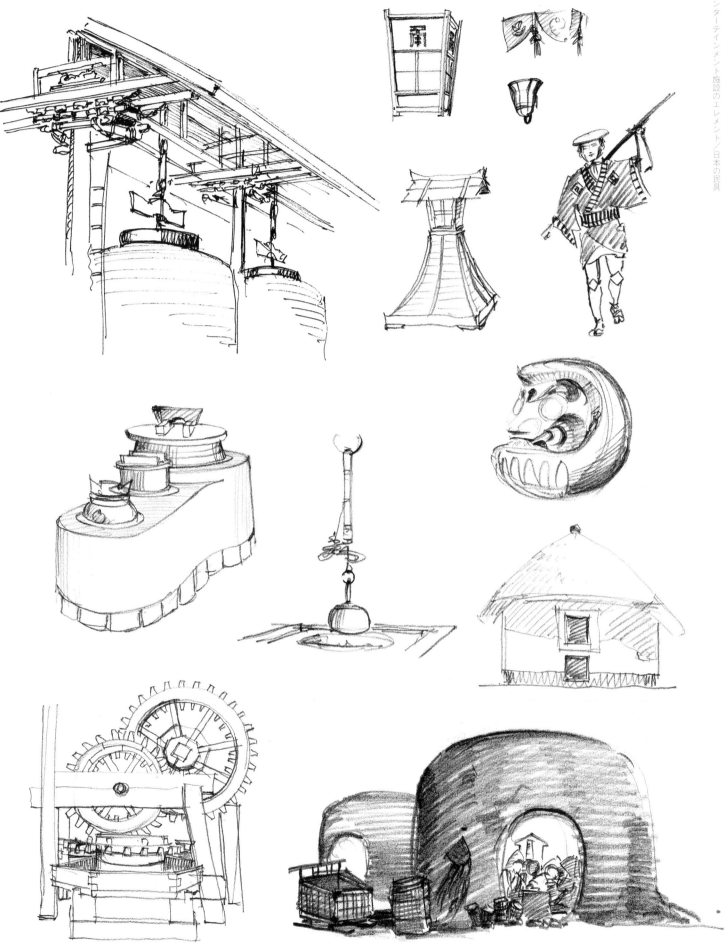

日本の祭り
Japanese festivals

ライドマシーン
Riding machines

キオスク
Kiosks

トリックと仕掛け
Trick mechanisms

コスチューム
Costumes

宇宙船
Spaceships

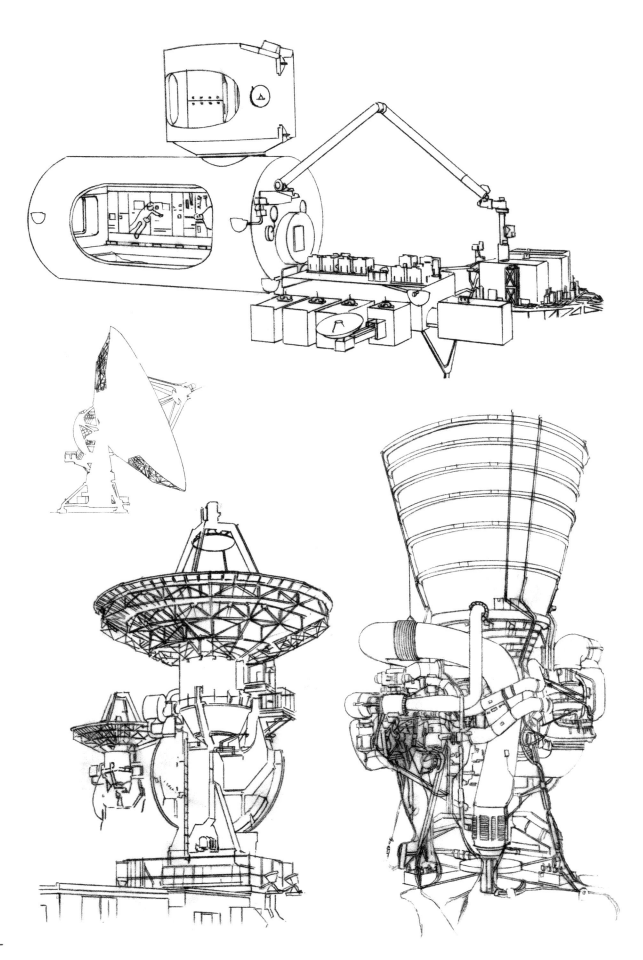

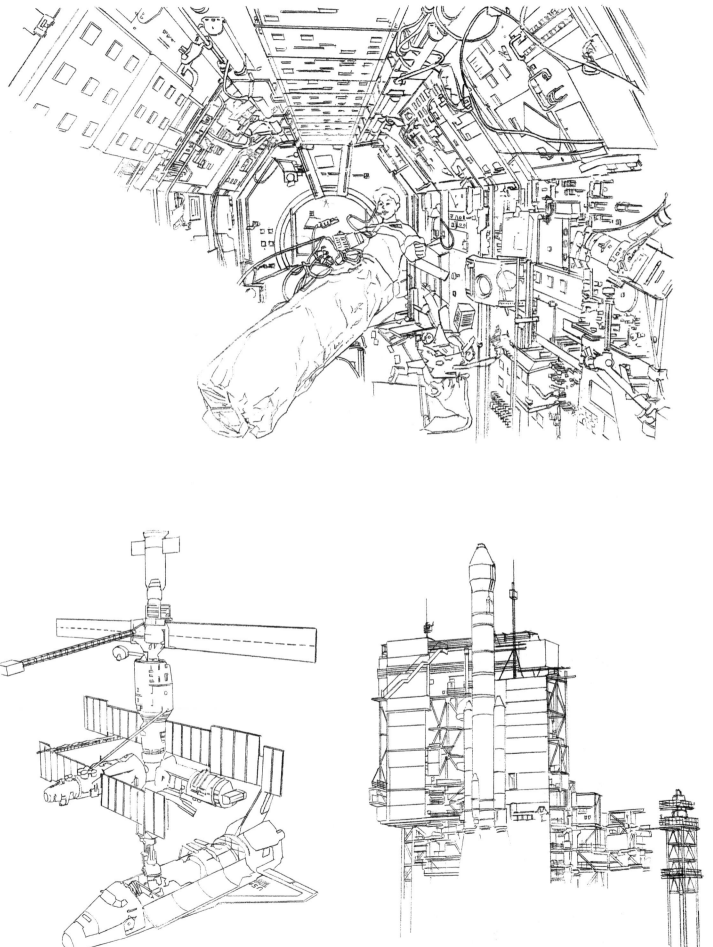

ペットキャラクター
Pet characters

ミュージシャン
Musicians

サーカス
Circus performers

謝辞

この本を作るきっかけを与えて下さった監修の宮後 浩 先生，また，作品として掲載のパースを描かせていただいた皆様と，出版にあたり，最後まで温かく見守っていただいた編集部のかたに心よりお礼を申し上げます。

著者プロフィール

仲田貴代史　Kiyoshi Nakata
1955年 大阪生まれ。
1981年 関西大学工学部建築学科卒業後，
(株)コラムデザインセンター入社。
宮後 浩 氏のもと，主に淡彩スケッチパースの制作と
企画部として建築関連のデザイン企画業務に従事。
1993年 仲田デザイン事務所設立。
以後も各種パースレンダリング，
建築関連のデザイン企画に携わる。
現在，仲田デザイン事務所代表。
関西芸術短期大学非常勤講師。

仲田デザイン事務所

〒542-0063　大阪府大阪市中央区東平2-2-1
大住協会館3-A
TEL(06)768-4347　FAX(06)768-3987

制作協力スタッフ

山下弘子，林 陽一，細井章子，中山文昭／仲田デザイン事務所
重村千恵／(株)コラムデザインセンター

監修者プロフィール

宮後 浩　Hiroshi Miyago
1946年 大阪生まれ。
1968年 多摩美術大学デザイン科卒業。
建築事務所設計部を経て1972年 コラムデザインセンター設立，
現在に至る。
(株)コラムデザインセンター，(株)コラムデザインスクール代表取締役。
近畿大学建築学科芸術学科非常勤講師。
日本アーキテクチュラルレンダラーズ協会会員，
関西インテリアプランナー協会会員，
大阪府技能検定委員。
著書に「インテリアプレゼンテーション」，
「イメージスケッチ」，「初めての建築パース」等がある。